hip twisted

a.j.l.

ISBN-13: 978-0-692-26380-8
ISBN-10: 0692263802

fewbluehue

cover by: a.j.l.

poetic reconstructions

7/25/2014

ACKNOWLEDGMENTS

21st Century Reference
Merriam-Webster
The Diagram Group / Skyhorse Publishing

CONTENTS

a.j.l.

To be read in any order wished;
front to back, back to center,
retrograde, skipped, or looped,
at any random page,
on any given group.

DEDICATION

Thank you all that are close to my heart.

My family: Constance Marie & Ben the Tiger,
Stephen D. & Kirsten V., Adina M. & Faith L. A.,
{*Csilla K.* K. love & *Sir* Sancho the *S*quirrel *S*layer &
*E*ccentric Mami}
-Joseph & Lisa M., Jios D., Ryan S.,
Brian C., R.R.R. & family,
Petrina & Peter G. & Mary J.-

44 sense

Consciously consistent church charities
are careless beyond any authority.
Antiquities significantly drop detonations
with the most sincere silence,
until the sirens of the city sound
low blown speakers in B minor tonic.

Revelate single sins in carbon cells,
and evaporate environments exceptionally well.
Believe in the bomb before the battle begins,
and we've lost our urge to kill once more.

Massive mistakes made us misunderstand
natures fury by design,
but all direction declined in systematic solutions by crime
through dynamic notice in pain of those tried.
Something takes its place instead of creating waste
that we would walk through without protection of plastics and
heavy materials made.

Once at last without a memory withstanding history
of memorials in modulations misplaced.
Never engaged, just as if they were erased,
and extensive evacuations became a lifelong project.

Lost contributions saved; trade erodes to worthless oil,
and predictably paid prophets expect
the even numbers to rise
in concrete markets of a new city.

Labors intense ignorance fell play to ratios
of stringing left over digits
that admit her patterns were wrong and too abstract
to attract favors of the decimals security;

prepared by evangelical enemies
before the erratic crash in evils game.

By any other name
it takes on new meanings of independence,
upon elaborate productions of impedance in speaker wire
made from the tired hands of Japan's traders.

When all is done,
and finished products parade the advertisers -
whom are shedding new light to proprietors empty eyes
in fluidity of green and silver;
it marks the last chapter delivered.

ph paper dolls

She followed destiny's path of violated attention
to be destroyed by psychopathic boys with foolish tools
of executed education.
It was a realization on part of fools who pretend to pray on top
of cheap concrete scriptures bought off E-bay.
Then came the feeling of being betrayed from her one and
onlys that skipped town next morning.

All alone without the practice of friends and family came out a
woman that is just a shell - whose mind became stormy.
Her cabinets of mood changing pills ceased its thrills as the
bottles lay on their side,
showing signs of lost instruction and pride.
Besides, she's wasted by her doctors game of insured lectures
and poisoned prescriptions that led from devious delivery of
tic-tic-tocks.

Toxic shocks take their time to synch with broken synapses,
buried beneath a trail of hardened hatred and sorrow.
Take it in by tomorrow and share the love with public affairs.
Jump on city streets screaming while pulling your hair.
The opportunity a bit rare, so we won't take advantage of your
time spent being ravage in the roads;
blocking cars and city buses by yourself,
all alone.

When the clock strikes eleven you wake up at home,
but don't remember the exclusive damage you've made;
being re-enacted and poorly staged right before your face.

When curtains fall into place between dry rotting spaces of
wood, starving termites terminate their world from inside her
bones - outside carved flesh neighborhoods,
only to leave soft cement stones.

Bizarrely broken homes of her youthful memories vanished,
once the legal poisons banished remaining theaters in the heart
of her brain.
A delicious pituitary gland is icing on the mental cake
once we create a final act of fate in pollutants.
Goodbye treason's of hate which give reason and states of
modified misery for eternity;
in complete dismissal and dismay.

when we feel *the urge* to be evil

Slightly different twisted ways we are in levels of the devil.

Yes.
To say we are complex is not an answer we can handle,
but rather a mythical fuck up.
Textural make up for men
made up into philosophical martyrs
sold by the pound in meat market sales
take pride with heavens glory,
and ungraceful bodies clutched to handmade bombs.
"Would you like the ribs, the rump, or the thigh?"
The suits watch in the butchers window,
and hang themselves with their corn blue tie.

Bounded mistakes on insurance claims
wipe away tears and sweat with dollar bills.
It takes in the thrill of beating gold digging woman covered in
plastic jewels - scraping their knees when pulled away from
ankles, kicking and screaming like
spoiled rotten children do
when told no to ice cream after dinner.

Before prayers come wishes,
and financial liberty in the big city to take care.
Profit before the ball hits you below that line
becoming unstable over time.
It drowns and drinks alcoholic thoughts when stressed
and severely depressed situations tossed around -
creating bruises with fractured bones, inside alone
Turkish tombs that Hungary kept as the great Ottoman slept.

Some escaped death, but under modern structure surfaced
ancient graves that Romans made with marvelous tools for
carving stones, and marble homes cross a path of skeletons.

Massive equal numbers holding children tight;
odds hold their severed head filled with fire ants,
nesting tunnels late into night.

Laid white eggs - align lower jaws when cracking soil
drinks rain water at $7.00 a gallon.
Corporate churches bought all oceans after *the great flood,*
now banking from the sales they made off Noah's family blood.
Believe me when I say it's the taste that we love.

It's not time to run from mistakes we've made
for future occupants that learn self flatulence,
before being able to speak.
Is it because of the wrong leaders we seek,
that promises difference in the way we feel and think?
Yet nothing seems civil when people balance their heart
with gold and silver linings.

Diamond studded pace-makers release Crystal when about to
feel the fall of another attack.
Once felt the glow of youth,
now waiting to pass away during great campaigns - pointing
missiles on heroes they wish to decimate in different states.

dropping sterile vases

Once I was on top of a skyscraper
that touched defective clouds to pressure,
until slivers of despotic-matter deviated above
my head in parabolic responses in measure.
Unlike a halo of perfected diatonics vanquished,
it dispersed like an erotically vitiated angel
who's never been handled by one to converge.

They sneak in your room to make love
while you dream the saddest ideas one could conjure.
The winds converse to high altitudes of reluctance
and distracted ambiguity.

Feeling the sadness in this *last apparatus;*
we commemorate an accident in the future sense.
It makes my neurons and torn transmitters extremely tense.
Thought I'd lose it – comes to mind of jumping off this free
ride with the comfort of impact points laid so richly below.
Until I noted that earth was only beautiful from a distance,
and ground zero had vacancy for the soul of one more.
So I decided to stay above the rest,
and gave that space away for someone else.

but! Alas! The earth is spinning so fast for that I feel nauseated
to the fact that I am only human.
The lure of your vomit hits envied faces of those behind you.
When rumbling under feet in foundations springs,
I followed the ones in front of me.

And from this building is spinning music,
of arpeggiated allegro to inseparable presto!
The frenzy handed antique instruments
with bow and strings next to a running chorus,
singing arias of ocean dementia against staccato trees.

Solid conversations on floor #1998 glue then bounce through halls - off walls to vibrate matter in the beat of god's heart.

The skeptics jump from windows on Newton's theories, as the piano lid drops on the hands to break the sound of his fucking romantic Chopin.

My flowers in this hour began to drop like polluted rain as vases fell up above my headache, until they reached space and time again.

eno pers id *rx*

My state of mind fascinates how long the weirdness persist.
World around me excites to exhaustive expansion
in 3rd person propaganda.
Tried to stop listening to myself,
and the other auditory verse went quiet.
I hate synchronicities when that's all you wake up for.
Are you sure it's the same as before?
This is not a self conceited war?

Hello June.

Unearthly weather drops to a ground.
Corns of alarmed locust remain an unbearable heat;
hot embers coiled in silver honey,
as I lay the trap for productive ants.

Excuse me for saying,
but there's too much fucking nature outside.
It puts my fucking strings on highly tuned tensions
of cracking faux wood -
grinding my teeth to the sound of my racing heart beat
in the dulling boredom of 5 point lunacy surround.

Life lays in axis between math and madness -
my apprehension from misconceptions.
Complete obscurity towards the apex near,
99% yearly exposure to radical fears.
I hate 37, 22, 13. Hope it's not what it means.
A depleted bottle of pills for my nerves;
still hysterical – is this what I deserve?
It's a summer of 3rd degree burns.
Too hot to be happy.
The time your closest ones turn,
it hurts the heart and burns compulsory.

May the devil make decisions with decadent designs,
deistic god revelations in contradictions aligned.

My balance off guard -
I can't tell from creation 1 to collapse of 0.
We make the heroes in centers between heaven and hell.
Mistakenly misanthropic - yes, we excel in purgatory well.

I must admit how indistinguishable the *two*.
How many levels of misery does one go through?
Hopefully not two hundred and twenty *two*.

Still can't wake ethicist love of atheist,
dejecting what's slovenly hated in seconds to years.
Times a houndrel of passive space -
triggety manifolds unsubjected and encased;
carefully spun resins in photolytic weeds of green.

First Impressions

Pulling ear wax from slippery putrid hearing canals is
something I like to see.
I drooled with foamy incisors;
indented in the holes of smelly cavities borne of
purple and green moldy discharge -
mucous traces in underworlds that stink of victims dying.
Looking wild and uncharted,
my mouth of horror came to stop you like a train wreck
as soon as I smiled wide with sincerity.

Intentions of the sincere suffer the exclusion of logic.
Now faith descends me twice on whether I've been among the
naughty and nice – the erroneous or precise –
into the blackened white cast of simulated light -
into superstitious separations turning time off a magnetically
coiled table.
I sat in the chair beside it.

Another smile made us pest.
The act of advanced gingivitis fermented in
ancient bad breath.
I soaked up saliva on my white collar and said,
"Got what she paid for I guess."

She tossed and turned on a silver lined mercury bed.
Poised inside by prophetic wet dreams,
preying memories in her delicate head.
And it escapes those who cared when the decisions lay on us
seductively posed -
softest to tightest muscle unexposed.
And as soon as shes fluxed in impossible positions by
increased force,
the over fill begins new poisons impregnated,
and they drip from the tired gaping slip.

Prodigious code came out in cyclopedic scrolls printed with
numerical text of sytemus punched papyrus.
But the jokes on us once again.
You can't read what is reminiscent.

Embrace what is over looked,

and unlearn what is wasted.

Yet we all hold variant keys in fractions of truths whole.

a'iphobia

1/Unclogging sludgy breeding nest in showers that won't drain;
touching wet malodour of unknowns
strait to the naked fingertip.

Don't think of what's hatched
to dictate your lowborn self.
It's you that you're touching all along.
You let it cod enough,
your disgraceful self haunts you.

The cell is a miracle birth,
and a mutiny of disease at the end.

Water creeps just above weak ankles wrapped in tasteless
transvested tissue tugging towards earth.
It's a strange page of mono-cycloptic strain and form.
Nasty civilizations reborn from humidity in a southern deep.

It crawls without disturbing shallow nerves.
A thousand greased, queasy larvae perpulating and pustualating
poxed pores.
Living tissue after death complete layers
to become you again.

Man or woman,
transgender,
asexual,
degenerate. . . .
just tall enough to shake your hand.
"I'm you, hello again."
Death to the doppelganger doo-doo!/

2/ My assholes douche string bear hugs the brain,
but without a penis puzzle it cannot be rearranged.

The thoughts so dull you'll be grinding gears in no fucking time
taking pictures of drywall to frame.
The inch is too small to live or escape. . . .
Hit the road but too many people exist.
Still, if I were the only one left,
I'd have steadfast panic attacks of the superego –
for one day, would you resist?/

3/Don't touch that!
It's been laying in the streets for weeks,
but it got pushed just like anything else.

… and every step of the way is just a step of a day.
Sixty seconds seems a long time to feel lonely.
A second ain't shit til you start to count them backwards when
you turn sixty-six.

I stepped too close to the crack by my feet.
Don't perspire too hard or you'll slip on wet concrete.
The gutter opened wide to exhale a sea of dead meat.
The aroma of falling flies the nose despised./

4/Get your greasy hands off my selector!
Twist selections in ties and reload breadboard switches aside;
a magnificent grid.
Yet, an optimal illusion.

Touched the selector switch and got greasy.
It said, "How's it hanging you bag of bones?"
thought the gremlins spawned inside with a funny glitch;
programming psych analyzed tricks.
One day used real science and got it fixed.

Code after code … how twisted you gotta be?
Punched in keys like a drum roll year after year./

5/I am a man, and the mosquito loves me.
Holy shit, how much can you eat, breed, and drink?
I feel on the brink with distraction in middle sea.

Arachnids are Splot blochemous - pushing northern fights.
With frenzy I'm stuffing fat in crevasses non-exist,
from the finger tip to the wrist.
Wallyballed in greased knuckles;
cracking under a trillhallidron complexifugue.

A hairy maldrex of effects upon the high-greed-pox.
It infects with microbilus in cum laden snot./

6/Trichypled nooses for your silence.
Lichen a statten brow drowning far off of me -
a riveted sixty-one/seven northwest degrees.
Encased diarevottus, where madmen plinth the disgusting
anodyne tock and transpondent temper tics.

An epiphany leveled the jitting-jots in precision cut lines,
but slap the face of a witch,
and your hand becomes useless grund.

Offspring flutter text possessively
til loops adorned long with odor;
sweaty panic attacks smelled dusted iron infusion.
They end, yet we are the forgetfuls./

7/My first awake spent screaming for hours.
My face hugs the pillow scanting deaseum antics til too tired to
wake for scathing days anew.

Waiting patience dulls times dimension,
in flat feet rolled to renal re-posits.
Itching each flinch of googolplex ocular ravings,
til blisters of crimson turn bristly purple.

Bugs can sense the notch,
revving central rings of buried rinky ticks.
Brings cyphus studders as ravaged sick.

Pushed a pill inside of me and pulled its position out.
Made rind broken worn -
more of a painful sight than touched.

I couldn't stop shaving pickled skin nor bleed out the rot.
As'tres muscles grouped to maffid meds -
hardening knit-nacking machinery of the synthoscopic sea.

. . . .

This is the product of mumbling nonsense;

madness is the key.

profauxde octavious

back-forth to tick-tock
left-right – revisiting mid-night
pendulum sway in gravity motion
deviously designed the largest wave from oceans

Cover the piano lid to protect your kids
as the roof of your home comes crashing in.
To-nights undertow, "Push out of what we rid."

The morning tide brings in the dead –
what we cannot hide.
Too many bodies back to send
no matter how hard we tried.
Each row we burn turns white ash,
embers of bone cannot last.

Unnerving as creative was destruction.
Windows slap hands whom do magic in
numerical dysfunctions.
"I think we're under attack by gods own neural inventions."

The loss of a blessing takes control
what we lost came back in pieces -
fragments told, "What we rid is what we're show."

The island riddled in macabre baroque misfortune.
Simple ownership belong to the dead,
under its wicked smiling sun.

Time still and paralyzed, I could not look.
I could not run.

Death sparks a vast choleric luminosity,
its residue buries the moon from atrocities.
Now we choose what to believe.

Inside, down below,
a copper wire corrodes through habitual flesh fires,
and cries drown out beneath anxious snapping -
decompression of foul air;
that unnerving razor crackling.

Daybreak marked weary shuffling,
a mass of tilted cedar structures in no design.
The endless view; a ground zero horizon
bound in pallid precipitation evoked.
A sea of debris over-tows the gulf -
expecting train delays every moment.

We waited til love came as gray dust,
showering the livings head and feet.
For most, left alone in the tropic heat –
nothing left for them but deathly dreams,
it was time to leave.

A new city turned remnants into old squatters,
after a 20th century plague of warm Gulf waters.
Trapped, transfixed between plyth and plywood -
lowest island in lungs last reprise.
Grave stones lost, new ones arise -
reminders of random population declines.

No matter the loss they raised again from incoming rain,
all is now drowsy;
tranquilized closely, carousing, forgotten, tame.
Survivors die, their children entrusted to livelihood -
a story by heart.
Of what was good, and what should have not,
in whole or in part.

Galveston 1900

up-*down*town/ reclusive states

Said, I've said it again.
The choice is never really a choice if done in second effect.
My sick head - some brain dead abused my boxed blue boozed
days behind you.

Living through this in mind I've signed off,
and became the rain with static on streets -
anti-supportive bleach,
and my car crashed through a truck
when the storm was over.

Dead, I did it again.
My life is never really over until the bullet hits the head.
My blue face with some halos grace sinking into motion of
ship wrecked oceans.

Living through this in mind I've signed on,
and became the trip star of satanic cars driving down the blvd,
and danced my pain away.

Said, and I've said it again,
the choice is never really a choice,
and actions are done in second effect.

A mad man; an intolerable man alone, but stoned makes a
bomb from materials he robbed in the past.
He swears he wants to make his genetic race last.

In effect the moon has the 2nd(dairy) effect today,
and tonight the sweet sounds of small feet create rampant heat
as they run across the forest.

Degrading out the white fine line to silver again;
a bomb and time comes so slow from a past,
but only love is the reason for this jaded path.

What peace had he made?
And to what ritual gain his indefinite displayed?

Gone again, and the mail is in the checking lane
with a wrong name to anonymity.

A bomb delivered by negligence,
and away goes a man to give his arms and legs.
The pretty bow and presence delighted a bright light of
chemistry to him.
A torso left for the media;
yet not the men of a little American government.

A redneck race riot is never right,
but alone in the woods is an old dirty laughing man,
shitting in his pants; waving his hands for the trade plane to
come by his home for more chemistry in his set.

below

When alone as kids we wished for better things.
Better times ahead as we walked the sunset street;
not saying it, but thankful to be alive and well.

Tales unfold wrongful truths
that create sadist moods
during childhood,
and the gypsy witches
with "lily white hands",
caressing the apple and diamond
that entices you in.
Be careful when you approach her step
for that it creeks from old weather,
and has seen better days and kinder nights.
She first gently takes your hand with delight
to the first step inside.
Then pushes you in a room far down the hall,
where no one can now hear you call.
 . . .
She crafts pinewood coffins in the attic
for children just like you
taking them off to a private island by the northeastern sea.
The old witch pays the toll boat,
"never let these souls free"
- the Bible at your head -
- the Testament by your feet -
final dropping grounds where the dead meet -
covered in prickly cotton from her most beloved,
"*fatal flower garden*".

Inspired by the recorded ballad: Fatal Flower Garden – Performed by
Nelstone's Hawaiians, 1929. Based on Child Ballad no. 155,
accounts from 1255AD, 5th century Syria.

balance

met a girl - now she's gone
looks like it was co-dependency all along.
thought about it and smoked a joint.
then put my head in the noose.
after all, "whats the point?"
a joke i told myself before i died,
but forgot it when all turned black.
didn't even try ...
to remember the name,
of the one who made me
want to die and go insane.

Last Dance in Ian Curtis

mr. oz was a man who did impersonations of a god.
mr. oz was a man who didn't give a shit,
who didn't give a fuck at all.
mr. oz was a man who never opened up
or revealed his coverup when defying odds.
he gave you two hearts,
a scarecrow,
then sensibility,
and false courage from above.

"the dance of a house with man made cyclones
will eventually fall to its feet."
i miss the cattle and the meat
with rotting carved fleshes off the bone.
i don't care where the blue cow has gone.
"all the strangers have left, but is this home?"

the roosters are not found in mourning;
the beef devoured viciously by low ufos.
everythings gone to hell while her aunt rings the bell.
supposedly a suicide in this photocell we presume.
an orgy of oily costumed cripples after
prescriptions consumed.
coughing blood with a cocaine password;
the stains of urine not technicolored,
still black and white,
and i cant understand how the prophet in
the prairie was right.

when nobody was calling for me today.

the tree won't throw apples if you step on the cracks,
but be cautious if you break your mothers back.

a lion wants to mar and rape a dog and his bitch.
a man of mercury swings the ax, but missed.
he wants to cut and cook her younger pieces
in his fiery stomach with cremated grease it releases.
a flimsy trotting rot of clothed straw comes with a song.
even if they would greet and bond,
that dog would never survive eight dancing feet
with a sing along.

Mr. oz was a man who did impersonations of a demigod.
Mr. oz was a man who didn't give a shit,
didn't give one fuck at all.
Mr. oz was a man who took your charly and your caps,
replaced them with angry tree sap.
makes you feeling monochrome,
then forgot to show you home.
you shout his name, but won't convert you back sane.
he let go in vain, left you alone, cold as the storm above.
your heart unfolds, turns to stone; leaving a most bitter love.

give her a ride.
give her a home.
give him some pride.
give him some bones.
give him a heart.
take what was shown.
next is the part
of what is unknown.

esloine

A girl saved a jar full of apple seeds
when she would painfully call it quits
The day came for a completion,
but instead she got real sick
Jolting aches to the spinal chord
forced her into a paranoiac trip
Inspects innocence through tolerations -
her perplexity of three pushing penetrations
Nervous nerves forced to a frenzy in tight twitching spasms
The ooze from worn vents warm towards intense
Confused muscles dance and give out
Organic slop rolling around greasy slots;
put back into position because it never stops
Her words turn to vomit in heavy phrasing
Persistent sweat of orgasmic nightmares sustaining
Joys violator runs love sick – making you the fornicatrix
The whiteness; insistent pumluggs dispose involuntarily
equipped

drip drip drap

Thick stick shlofts a distal loose quiver
Altruist faces forlett in forty five
Flays a ducks-worth in malid meat
Sway prescriptions to playful punci palidrads
They stink and sweat sacred osculation –
plenty winflous to beat til sweet

She is a wounded silver stud on another woman's tongue
Slippery slutting in soft focus macro runs
The reproducer loose and thin
Out escapes the moisture's heat

A cry out, "Perpulate me, then exchange!"

The esophagus is the start of a salivating tunnel
Every seventh to tip, rudely protruding organ
Makes her hiccup

Passing&Rantings first person collect calls aharmonically
expelled

Crafty triangles reflex in and out
A magnus fluxing of skin draped on bones
It glistened micro visions under un-natural light
Time clocks hard fleshy hands past imaginary midnights

Smoothest muscle turned numb
Abused a wear-out
Puffing sounds exhausted from trapped air
Too tight, too dry before something gives and tears
Limits are the key
Well, we just wait and see

On your hands and knees, head hanging off the bed –
deeply pray for me again and again
Voices invidiously say, "Let's begin!" …
repeated those rambling phrases, though she couldn't read an
idea branded by supernumerary abuse

They slipped in a slippery half-turn
Moebius stripped; trisecting a churn, protruding cages of ribs,
spinal tri-tetra astern
Recycled sweat and cyanide dreams of infinite return,
they come yet never go
This insists to be a repeating show

circumstance dance

please don't break the chair -
endless sitting stares at the past
take my hand, stand, and dance
all our precious clocks timed wrong
to the offset vinyl song
skipped a note with one in your name
tonight there is no pain - only us

your flowers became the hour
when all but time was fixed
into the bruise -
wearing down our shoes
as we fell on the dance floor
but please don't break the toys -
because tonight there is no joy
only us

then only us becomes only me
only me *descents* not to *three*, but none

there is duality in this dance
if too blessed and righteous inside,
an external miserable force abides
if absolute evil is your mind,
a stride in prosperity slaps you kind

balance breakfast on the table -
a prayer and old fashion self affliction
must stand –
broke the chairs when withdrawing addictions

true that times goes fast when *compos mentis,*
yet the clock appears broken in *annus horribilis*

off the wall in destinations
hanging myself with an expensive tie
let out that final breath as a given sign
to tell my prostitute goodbye
before she left me for the city

she caught attention as a dancer
i secretly went to see her every run

she spun around in bound feet
showing off when all fill the seats

a ballet of obtrusive pain in natural light
soon an accident looses sight

no applause when you're not pretty
too many choices in massive cities

lost the chords to take fake flight
wings of madame butterfly
gets hold of you when she bites

spreads the illness through acoustics
repulsive stances heart a reclusive

private eye to pervert
one whom seeks dominating servants

Malifphant

Typhoid circus numerator for open circuit isolator.
Standard in the front, greedy in the back.

Byte up – *I am of love and whores*

Kept slamming the ass with input and quarter-bales of grass.

Back to frantic times in fractional jaded pace;
strictly comforted with lips, eyes, ass, the hips,
and strings of theoretical ethics on the Rhine.

I can't deny you. . . .

May-the-devil crossroads once for your case -

exposed for another ride when loaded with *those alcohols*.

Your chess is evil
Those moves too aggressive
-Damn you-

You are my queen, but you took that too.

I did not want to inherit that evil,
but did under your navel thrice.
"Oh boy" how I listened to that pearl every night I could.

It sweats heavy grease, leaving stains on the pillow to stingy
ankles opened without ease.

The smoothest loose taking, then giving out.
How far does a tight absence go?

A pretty eye with too many lashes to count,
opens at the pupil
< in and out >

I stole your knight that night.
...panting and grunting – tail twitching left to right...
Set a trap in the rear of the castle when you didn't look,
then your queen swung and shook.

Cleared a way through vertical moves.
Csocsi's with dandytattyspot spit, slides off applied lube.
Bouncing, coconut scented oil rig;
digging further down every day.
It really hits a sensitive nerve.
Fast, slow, exotic shutter speed combinations;
No lock, Never a Key to relieve aspirations.

ursulator

The strangest of paradigms:
a eukaryote decline.
For them, a post requius quintet written -
under shored below the Macron Mass.
Intoned recluse, mechanically seared its minimizer for parts.
Composed instructed blank phrases in hermetic blood for
starved pianos, percussion, and drop repeater in E,
added a dry contact in A.
fade forth response to be far talk,
close microspeak for a dead on collision -
starts to rain binary transmission ahead.
Aluminum leaks scream a duet with its closest friend,
"Le mano, La ci darem"

Kafka laughter & the harmonious pig.
Don't strike the bass drum too hard and break the skin,
or a tiger will jump out and begin to attack, then kill.

The stage crumbled underneath over-mic'ed performers.
Third act down by standing upper gallows deemed unstable,
towards notes not known in events of lesser tones -
trapped extinctions inside ancient reflections before a past.

A beauty vantros of silk and
philharmonious funeral behavior.
Arranged long gutted strings across the mouth of a little organ,
nailed against the room.
Plucked when air wheezed out the box of sticky keys.
Added more tuned wires across holy floorboards
to above the rafters.

A masquerade in geometrical fantasy,
obscure sight of another worlds martyr.
Earths first foreign crucifixion,

another germs ethical starter.

The terminative era concert held aid before a riot,
theater was already a folly.
Every almshouse came to us drooling down,
up from stilt shifty battens unsound.
Cautiously prepared empty patters for the aleatory chamber
test, tones in C-ten,
a solo synthesized phoneme selection.

Drop repeater lowered pressure to sink advanced amoebus
down reconstruction rinks.
Low E rounded from three to seventeen.

The most sincere concatnetive diphone speech sings through
anacynical garbled engines,
and ring mod fragment machines.
Articulatory analytica technologies fornicate and reproduce,
making dumber chips construe lexically boozed.

Defunct-degenerate drums and flunky piano under-loose
saddens a silent body.
The face of advanced syphilitic stages stand upon a
Schubertesque soliloquy symphony.
Eyes on the crowd of crows feet stepping stupors to new notes.
Lines narrowed up to semiquaver point nine triple time -
less than half quarter tonic frames of mind.

entertainment contract 1na-cl2

try, start, try, fail,
intoxicate, start, succeed,
intoxicate, try, start, fail,
try, fail, try, succeed,
try, succeed, intoxicate, succeed,
intoxicate, start, sell, succeed,
chronic intoxicate, try, start,
addiction intoxicate, try, fail,
try, start,
cell, fail,
try, start,
addict intoxicate, try, sell, fail,
no control intoxicate, try, start, fail,
eliminated intoxicate, die, sell,
success, loved, martyr,
sell, ashamed,
sell, forgotten
rotflmao
lmao
lol
ha
eh

closed *instruction* loop

It crept up inside our ears and ass.
We loved the music machines made.
It's not natural. Foreign and invading -

a malice pestilence you create.

The black electric boxes did what was told,
and for as long as they could hold a current.
Privately perverse programmed percussion's
pronounced pretentious profoundness and penitence -
bi-polar if running too long.

I think I like it more when absolute contrivances disappoint.
I think I love the contradiction as its value is slightly human.
Once in awhile we had to event parricide when the
transmitter was not treating their black plastic slave correctly.

My psyche is disclosed, for someone who pretends to now
want love, but I do.
Listen to the insanity I've created,
yet you find my mechanics of auditory repute romantic.

This is the *art* of *zero* when unmanageable emotions make
nonsense to *noise*. It's the *art of naught*.

Atonal transmutations obfuscate the real numbers again.
It's alright really, because I think I like you too. You love my
distorted drums in decimated dial tones - noisy tape loops that
keep clicking beat players in circular rings. My wall of
complex textures in simple articulated seeds.

You get high and lay down.
You think it's what the body needs.

Girl you're insane.

Show me some skin or get the hell out of my room.
This is not the place for people of average assume.
This is a jungle of savage;
a place I've found to loose my ways.
I tried to be as destructive as my sounds allowed,
but I too glitched under monotonous repetition
of teenage repressions.
So she took off her top, and I silently panicked under a dense
sound of vibrations to hide the fact of sexual uncertainty,
but unlatched her bra to hasten opportunity further.

Logan came out from his steel trap home-garage after huffing a headache of deleterious fumes. Triad of wet computers - the seeds of moisture setting silently in the windows you own. Hot spark ran up gallons of lurid sweat, bossed around too much and ceased to operate.

He restarted towards a hotbox.

skip .. skip .. skip to my lew my darling
Objects in motion –
crease a needle be damaged on recurrent memory,
will twiddle sadly during panicked bastardy devotion.
spin--spin little bastard spin--

I applauded his rustic achievement - hitting the drum machine's claps button that hung on plastic chains from my neck. Logan would assure the beat box would be doomed for abuse. Years later in 98' he eventually "cut the fuse".

When you can't afford the machines, make them yourself.

It came as a construct junk heap that sparked every power on.
Sometimes the jolt up the arm from shitty data in convoluted
ROM.
Triggered typeset keys in phonetic speech,
hammered themselves inside-out towards overheated
polyphony preaching.
Pin needles pushing to bent heads pound and fix in silly
traumatic shavings of flaked lead.
Symbolic punctures inside its vessel of faint
inwex transmissions –
a random shitty MIDI system sewage dump exclusive.

Programmed heads jammed with dirty grease;
depressing distonal clusters that are unable to desist –
a sound heard for blocks that foreign ears resist.
The temperature rises to the smell of failing electrolytic caps,
springing a sticky menace from fabricated mishaps.
Micro psychonic pulse in angry match-head rhythms -
another land mass in shifter strikes.
The break – crashed jots with wray-ray's run up,
and phallicious phuck-ups.
Chromatic romanticized ensembles
synchronize unstable pitches;
a symmetrical crime in clarity.

A gross pressure fizzled out long hissings of IMB fluids;
snakes midnight ready for adynamic amplified cross-kills -
it never surprises me on the half-life of cheap machines.
We live and diet

We stuck our fist in oily vents to reach a climax.
The mouth of the machine gated open;
expelling psychoactive steam.
I took a deep breath to collapse at the door.
No awaking from your dreams

lines of sugar

i slept with the queen who wanted my head
she carried a jar of bees with honey and bread
i ran far away from her nest that got the best of me
on my way making love with a million gypsies

then the worst came to floor us
when all the bees flourished
from the forest brought a misery
that made gypsies dance in viscosity

one by one a thousand stings in all
just to see the truth fail and fall
is it any wonder? why i wonder.
that today is the worst ive ever felt

when the place fell to pieces i looked around and asked
"what does she want with me?" i left the dead and passed
so once again i was all alone in bed
no one to hold closely - not even a queens head

then i woke to find her bees at my door
knocking furiously to every step i take on the floor
ill never give the honey back to her fleet
instead i drank it and forever went to sleep

one by one they won the fight
just to see if truth fails to light
is it any wonder? why i wonder.
that today is the best ive ever felt

dedicated stranger

Oh those acrostic times we live when sleeping.
Pouring out what we can, but not a soul takes note.
Thoughts excused better than dreams, til the turn of
equated edges fill emptiness with flogging despair.
The next miss-match unannounced, unrepaired.

These sarcastic illusions are killing me.
Wake to shake fidgety obsessions with nervous cells. . . .
feeling of return from a catholic hell.
No halo seen but a trinity unveiled.

I am misconception.

If only someone would speak of reality,
leaving truth to mundane hands in fantasy.
Balancing acts not possible as tested,
but every sixth month,
unconscious allow flight.

I always think today the world will cast last shadow.
Post-requiem preconceived, past, present, in one hour;
constant simultaneous lives vibrating golden frequencies.

A collector of ink blots in a negative self esteem.
A collector of staples hits them on target from velocities
impaled between four fingernails.

Sleep sleep sleep – bones brittle, muscles weak.
Shred of meat tied loose to snap weighted plates of liver.
The accounted masses held ceremony, acted as selfish maggots
eating a way home to DMT's empathy.

The freeze in circular heat hits ravenously mean -
pestilence pissed off.

We do the best flaunting -
cut delusionary distances into quotidian fractals;
a moment of time beat with warm hostility to the face,
as areas involved hold tight blistering embraces.

The tremble aftershocks of a city mad, collapses ideas of
thought along with cannibalistically created tunnels.

Dreams of new doors dead ends inside mazatic architecture.
Closed-in escapes activates strait stairs on the flat floor,
leading to taller walls of disillusioned blank halls anticipated.

My greatest love whispers melodic lines until undisguised.
The execution of hope before memory despises to rope -
a thousand feet of heavy lies beneath her noose of ice.

Betrayed by my brain to think there is no causality in travels.
Time is always a river no matter how un-balanced.
Slumbering between forks, my obsessions unravel.
Terrified of new forms of matter.

I fall further than before into repeats of pattern,
with wishes never to be fully granted.
How much can I mentally spare when shaking this lantern?
Though, being awake, life too reflects the disenchanted.

girl with the crown

It's been so long that I don't remember a thing.
So long that I don't remember a past, but fragments.
I don't remember a name or hold the patience anymore.
It's been forever since I've put myself together I record.

You look of someone that has the sense of common wealth
with encouragements of the *devil in your lonely details*.

It was up in the sky when change came about in a contrast of
cumulus clouds, claiming controversy to those whom paid
attention.

She came crashing down in her mortal body of
bruised flesh and tired bone.
It was her crown that kept her up with unpleasant hesitations.

Her head rained hard on the desert, bringing life to ahead,
but her feet soaked poisonous blood into the ground, killing all
existence from her crown - what we cannot control.

Have we lost an inner beauty,
an internal symmetry to deprive simplistic joys?
Even with her answer, we did not take them to face
unscheduled fears by prophetic patrons' words of judgment.

We keep saying, "Don't blame us for bad decisions",
but is this the best we can do?

x to y: y do you know what you know,
from the dirt, to your face, from clouds to the sky?
The fire – it burns the ground you stand on;

Burns the buildings you live in

 Burns you alive

  Give me a glass of water before I die

Neighborhoods just one big shit heap
    Dropped before an array of sounds
    A storm in the darkest part of night
        Starts from zero, an empty space marked down

My organs vibrated violently,
my insides wanted to shut down;
my heart wanted to stop to a pounding halt.
Then terror hit me completely when noises became unbearable.
Nothing like any sound I can relate to -
then stopped suddenly,
every low tone at once.

It was so shallow then swallowed me whole.
The words started to hurt my stomach,
and a headache came up above the head.
My blood pressure remains the same,
but this pressure tears apart the muscles of my heart.
It makes me hold tight and fight for another hour or so,
but water stretched too far away to hold my people.

I tried to carry the one who kept that lie up,
and persistently said the truth was somewhere in between
our level of understanding - the core of birth til death.
The facts were there before a short breath of a storm came -
dissolved letters made of deep sugar cane
lined with fractions of fiction to the smallest grain in tact.

tape

mechanisms involved revolving levels
of demagnetized heads once curtained in chrome,
laying fragmented catalog in resins imprinted;
dried decade dust stains, left a lone silhouette.
the reader had fast flattened teeth - incessantly clicking,
cutting like a contemporary guillotine on edge.
one is exhausted inside to obtain maintenance
during contention – warmed from the heat of breath.
the energy alone burns the sun out from your eyes.
three restrain transformation in temporal ways
for what lays trapped within, phonation inside.
five interpolated cultures of the last order:

An Inexorable Rite.

why does irregular certainty declare
an analogue revolution recorded?
relinquish my faith for what lays amused
in six centers of a number nine hell.

audibly adequate apparitions aroused
an alarming apparatus aware,
and antagonistically abject.
its origin from nature –
started as simplicity ends the wreck.

as the tape turned, came a heavy hissing
that became the air around us.
inhaling speaker signals bruised the brain
enough to imprint atmospheric ozones -
past perfects touched privately
by wasteful interrogating interference.
then to the lungs it has its effects.
it seems the project finally begins the test.

voices low inside white noise whispers nasty words
within the movements of sensitive volume needles.

no secret in comments left guesses
for questions not worth asking.

we listen in real time to what was once linear;
in kinder lines, waved worded transfigurement.

it quieted the room to a sadness.
it surrounds with chemical lust
as out dated electronics get the best of us,
and the magnets scream to a teeth biting halt.
we packed what was ours and said,
"goodnight. don't let your memories bite.",
and memorex never sounded so real,
after you feel disaster.

the paradoxibolaholic

"The warmest rush I have lived since birth slows to dance,
leading paths inside others:
infused knots of photosphere anxieties –
unknown principle properties.
Stand if I can when the bend of light is just right,
turning shrouds into spirits, wine to wheat,
eastern grass to poly-glass."

In check; some turn sinning saviors,
others detest their past,
I fear the future,
more won't handle the present.

/The one who detests all time built an antenna
High into heaven, the grounding low to hell
It sparked in-between a creators passion
& moral along unwavering pitched hums
New generators sang in calibrated chorus

Man-made lightning revolted to fewbluehues
Unpredictably safe; he slowly walked through
A frozen electrical storm rapids in discharge
Cold fusion flowers cleaner than arctics parabola
Tasting for a high tension trigger

Magnetic vortex getting too hot
Graphite slivers squeezed away
Drilling new holes for bolts not yet built
Release is exposure flat-lining away without apologies
A composure of weighing closure/

/He wanted to change the world
But it changed him as well
Wanted to create as much freedom as tyranny

Tappings in cipher to deliver outer beings
Tore down his unearthly towers
After they turned night into day
A reckless mind dreams of being king/

/A notice how secrets transmute
Before they fade and die
No longer my words
How unkindly intentional lies
A scoff of five wise men won
Declares both tragedy's humor/

/A peaking fall in solutions derived
Smoothest slide against the hypersonic sounded collision
A math of dust conceive curvacious longing
Inside consumed vacuums cubed

When all made sense, it caused his face to permanently sneer
Divergent unorthodox spouts as if an endless auctioneer
He suffered enough excretions
Silk plasmas like last flopping fish
Descaled to the main fin/

/He's angry at a world he wanted to help
Thought up ways to make it hell
Fixations firmly grounded across impacted forest
Misdirection amidst the earthly tourist

Bound black holes beneath white hills
Expunge unequaled insanities
Halt the bridge a proximity sways to
Condensely bent inherent frequencies
A non-fluent foundation laid
But we never believed
A damn thing he would say/

False rapture blues

It wasn't God, but what happened was sad.
A sticky panic of breath stuck on window panes -
take out Chinese with church symbols.
Give out MSG to little Halloween children.
They wear mask and elastic hats
Armageddon style with a fake Hitler mustache.

Got fresh orange juice milked from farmers daughters.
They grow unrestrained here in the south,
just like the *girls gone wild* tree species.
Get it for $19.99, bonus DVD about a mouth.
Then wear this GGW-tee in public. -
every parents nightmare gone heartsick.

Bling a ring - Blah blee blah
"and let me do what i need to do
that's all i ask of you,
and that's all I *hate* to say,
if heaven doesn't want me
then all i have to do is pray."

But don't you be masturbating when heavens debating
to reach its hand for yours.

A dilapid brothel of nippers slut-a-mess.
We've exposed their nanneral pit excretion nest.
Pestilence aside, preachers lock every door,
and inflamed every level of children inside.
A list of mandatory magistrates hang outside,
retaining a list of names - only trace they were ever alive.

The minister has 5 minute lunch breaks.
He smokes a joint before going to heavens gate.
So saddle your children down,
and ride them into town.

Everyone gets a free chance with boys,
and robotic cheap plastic toys.

Wear your finest spurs today.
Tie and tape sharp knives to the ankles -
it's pretty faithful to make *them* disabled.
Now sit tight when pulling these cables.
Tomorrow comes a wonderful Christmas eve;
but it's the twenty third, so you're my pony,
bleeding at it's hands and knees.

mad man at werk

Man - a simple man who frowned down on his
subliminal smiles went though dials on phones,
and faxes - sent damn bloody taxes returned.

Walking away he saved the day for rain that brings more time,
and fucked faced rhymes in cryptic hip-hop music he uses
to break disastrous weather conclusions inside complex crimes.

Damn the atomic clock after 7 because of its high potency rate.
Be polite with machines that malfunction in different states that
take in complications of communications with delinquency.

Figures that rocket above the graph can't calculate the distance
equally within another trap.
Mythical binary root of misplaced sequences,
unbalanced below point three digit probability.

He thought, "This is silly!"
While at the end of the hall with a metal baseball bat -
a home run that season;
smashing with reason all computers to pieces that fall.

we *be* gone

I awoke on the 22nd and made the mistake that we were
alive and well in a caged dwelling of a cities past,
where the blind made encrypted messages of revelation braille.
A fat ass doesn't hesitate about eating the stale wedding cake of
ambassadors missing - all along a trail of pity that tears once
soiled where dogs went pissing - now remain with crushed
bones of bodies boiled from their skin,
and lipstick smudges still alive during rain fall each year.
Radio towers disassembled laid each half mile end
when transmissions suddenly went missing.
And again, dangerous electrons danced from the sky above our
dead to celebrate infected skin in streets,
a reminder of what lays ahead.

In a dark empty cellar bed we passed time, drinking and
smoking vegetable, killing troubles in our weary minds.
Making close friends with black mold takes a toll from where
you're living as the strange black cat won't stop its midnight
hissing.

I took my daughter in my arms and carried her out in a
frilly white dress that now became dark from
sitting on ashes while playing on burnt decks.
I found her staging a last tea party with two elderly guest.
When about to grab her and tell them,
"Sorry for the trouble." -
I looked at faces melted with fire during fear.
They spoke softly with eyelids sealed shut,
"No trouble or worry sir.
She's a dear!"
I couldn't stop noticing they no longer had noses nor ears.
Even with no way to see
they turned their heads towards me,

and tried to smile while sipping cocktails and
expensive beer as we walked quickly and quietly
to the nearest hill.

We sat down and saw the closest sea.
It gave me frightening chills.
Once filled with water and life; now a deep desert engulfed by
self impaled skeleton sharks, tankers rexed in oil rigs,
and whale flesh that's mechanically seared.
I've never been so nervous about the ocean until now.
It was a garbage dump display of museum quality.
Its trash was never ending in horizon as the heaps of bleached
bones created mountains of living nightmares and macabre
ballet.

My daughters hand held tighter each time she felt frightened
with true engaging fear and enduring dismay.
She wasn't nervous by accident when we came across a
cruise liner laid to its side.
Wouldn't be surprised if no one survived
this upside down cemetery can.
I held her tight and ran down by the side of a breached hull.
When we decided to sleep that night it was unbearably cold.

I awoke to the sounds of silence.
Not crashing structures or breaking stone with metal,
but the smell was awful;
getting worse within each minute of the suns dials all fixed.
My daughter woke and asked if that's the smell of
people dying.
I'd be lying if I said, "No, baby."
Then again,
I really didn't know for sure.

We walked the wretched mile of decomposition with
wide open eyes,

becoming dry and irritated by high heated reflections
to wavy mirages; engraved in small shattered glass,
once sand.

In shaky hands I hold my daughter,
walking deeper every 13th step aligned
to lower altitudes history passed.
Getting weak. Getting tired very fast.
Being afraid! … Trying to pray and seek a better life.
When all is gone you begin to entice the idea
that your priorities lay all wrong.

My daughter and I stumble stupidly further as steps
became slower; the center of earths gravity pushing and pulling
closer to demise.
She dropped quickly; breathing in nitrogen enriched perfumes I
exhaustively exhaled.
We reached a deeper sea made from over flowing oil spills.
Black as our eyes turned toward the meanest hell.
Efforts drain the dream I had on the 21st into this
privately perverse wishing well.
Crude misjudgment on my part played a point at every stage
with unconcern.
All errors without a single thought to what she said during
every un-repaid turn.

Cat hallucinations

When I put flea repellant above his shoulders,
Sir Sancho the Squirrel Slayer went crazy with disorders.
The box stated not to get in an animals eyes or mouth,
but still had mad visions in a pyriproxifen rain-out.
He moved with aggravated twisting and spasms -
oddest meows with no hint of sarcasm.

Eccentric little Mami stares,
but sees something completely different.
All that appeared above her head went excitingly fast in
quizzical motions.
Sir Sancho no longer craved devotion,
after all wicked witches melt in petroleum.

The painful little flea fuckers
joined the circus next town; my socks.
I was curious with fever parasitism
performing all you can eat on me.
No stopping the slapping of my head
to pulling day old scabs off the edge
towards new infectious bites.

My legs covered in fresh to dry blood
under geriatric dress socks -
covered my calves of carnivorous love.
They hid within the fibers;
creeping, crawling, burrowing, fucking,
eutherian feeding – never asleep, forever aggressive.
Continuous hunger – always angry, a constant wake,
always a war inside your skin.

I picked my nose without washing off tetramethrin.
Lucid burn of nickle plates trap inside bored nerves.
Stranger than fact or fantasy; I didn't feel a debilitating high.

Knelt over to dry heave a nest,
only hornet eggs snuffed out.
I have a host of retarded brain cells,
felt-up nose hair traces offended.

The anti-flea box turned propaganda on me,
asserting images of badly drawn parasites in a death smile.
Stillness to Hyper Insecticidal warfomercial hours on end.
Colorful words braze excitement in super rad fonts;
jumping off the box like super friend crayons writing,
"We kill the best, and with a buzz!"
Made war a twenty minute indoor hobby,
soundtracked by lame, lousy thoughts;
persisting odd hard-ons' hang out during wrong times.
I decided it was my turn to put repellant on my shoulders.
That was my moment of flea head trophies, chemical glory.

It makes my skin wince to think …
War in between the walls.
War outside your home, inside your car,
between your roads and tires.
Car exhaust fogs to fight the clean.
Cat launches, and doggy jumps over dead zoned doo-doo.
Flea leaps on human hairs; invaders to disease our vitality.
Wars globally - microscopically.
Hand sanitizers, antibiotics, flea sprays, and prayers.
Good gracious we gag joppers with spoons,
to doggy slaves in slavish roehbox.

Before ramblings about war I slipped around in dress shoes,
and socks drenched in household artillery,
but they kept jumping harder and higher.
They attack as quickly as theirs is received.
I was getting happy hard; horny and headaches
in temporary misty clouds of delicious perilous vapors.

Battles against the fleas
And the remainder of me
Was given zero sympathy

I'm tired of all this! 'combat-ready fighter jets';
I may have better things to do?
Yet it's hard to stop once you start destructively.
… they feel absent from any virtue and integrity.

The poisoned blood rushes to my brain.
I am now one with the mystical cats,
of reptilian consciousness;
a side of self induced chemical killings.

People I haven't seen in years appeared in
forms of apparitions as if they were dead.
I talked to myself with a jitter in my voice
until one of the ghost reconversed.
Radio flash, every cat in my past; comes alive;
playing in concentric circles that made
Sir Sancho hide in damp cabinets.
Purple Mami stares close at white walls.
She gazes hard, but can't comprehend.
It could be anything haunting her exclusive stare,
but she sees what she wants.
Most likely years worth of canned wet food in a devastating
pile up;
opening to a naive leap devoured by Purple-Mami-Piranha
teeth,
or a thousand banshees converting to cannibalism,
or the bumpy ridges of lead paint messages within.

Bloodsuckers insisted and persisted the fighting.
I'm in solitaire with a can of empty pesticide;
breathing the last wheeze of whippets – *the new air.*
But I'm pissed this shit happens when the weather is fair.

the patio

God – opened the door earlier –
this awful stench of rotten smells.

It was like a mixture of piss and mouthwash expelled from a
league of mouths diseased, gums bleeding.
That lingering odor unforgivable by god and all glory.
The breath of a man whose teeth decayed to the very bottom of
the nerve, and spread a deep color in turning bone.
Morbidly horrid images come to mind of broken jaws,
shattered enamel shards that protrude rudely from deep rotted
indention's - what infestation left behind.
Hanging nerves dangle out non-healing dry socket holes that
stink of garbage dumps in August.

I swear I tasted the smell of soaked molding cardboard that
holds the urine like a honeycomb of delicious flavors.
A familiar smell you get used to in a middle school
boys room.
Standing piss on that unelevated ceramic floor -
your feet can't hide from it.
Once that sticky noise hits your ears from expensive *Nike* shoes
it's over. All over.
The odorous residue from classmates penis holes
that won't stay on restroom floors follows you home,
and next to your bedroom pillow it starts to grow.

Where was I?

Oh yes.
The little flies.
They started to collect more frequently in my pile of
soggy cigarette butts.
New vaccines available it seems,
and by all means a steaming pile of sin for all to see.

We were waiting till August to film that scene -
wiped it down without our hands.
Make it kinda clean enough.
Every corner was painted in sloppy strokes.
A wasp nest still rests between slits that
lead to dilapidated space.
Once an oozlious delatrid vent is now stuffed
with petrified dust.
Combs of a delicate thread hangs overhead,
painted over in a humorous lust of poisoned stings.
The civilization once strives a larvae for self defense.
Its abandonment left myopic visions immense.

/ 21 dead fly's on their backs along the breaker of scenic
screens – surrounded by trapped spiders looking for some cold
comfort – in collection where warmth designs.

Exhumilate in force-able circles to centrifuged blood -
plasma cells don't procreate livid,
a lavish ruin of the tug.

The feast is devoured deep in pulsating colons,
in-lined with secondary teeth.
Foulcynic scents trail back invalid wind.
All those deca-metric joppy joints humping stiff necks with
intent of injections.
Watch for the *lux dire*.
Germ fatigue and ill-weighted. /

Ardent adversaries duplicate then hibernate.

They are now indoors too. They hide in the sink.
Little box full of kitty dumps are alive inside with butt-worms;
near black mold tiles that's been in standing water for years.

Opened the cold door – few came out from twitching fur that was once called food before. Apartment kitchens always led me to a *steady diet of nothing.*

Larger living groups of invading species like ourselves are hungrier, and quickly goes my stomachs audio pattern that unsettled down and through.

Drink the decomposed vegetable until you can't feel it creeping deep. Pass out in colorless vomit to wake when the sun becomes anew.

But I felt like fucking shit, and went right back to a better sleep. Awaited a new day when not feeling so dark with miserable blues.

withdrawal

... and a bruise came with a drop in the same days sun.
she held a *familiar* close to her chest -
me a needle, and you a noose.
i'll be damaged, you be goods.
so who's talking to whom?
i'm too much a wreck to converse with you.

- ring around the poppy seed -

time to hide opiates under the bed
in the smoothest cigar box cut close to ahead.
bubbling spoons cut romances in two then powder.
that boiling heat from utensils got much louder.
be aware of remarks you have made -
the drop of lower eyelids post a recurrence.
a fever of smoke when you drown to sleep,
dreaming under currents slow to attack a threshold creep.

hello, today's a new day.
have something new to take away this pain?
there's not much time left in a twenty-four.
she quickly answered "no" then ran away.
now im pissed as the sun gave me cold shoulders,
then showed me the door.
i withdrew the syrup by twelve pm,
and saw things i rather have avoided ...
yet it haunts my afternoon and i soon remember in deosil ...

"*You*'re my lover & my junkie,
and nothing can ever break us apart.
bruised and blue and bright through light and
canned in blank and stuck in dyke,
devil's greased string and strapped with hope on songs
and smiles with grungy rope."

i woke with a cold sweat now married to the
molecule instead,
but the fever is holding strong and
wants and waits for me dead.

they come in singing low,

"dead presidents holding hands with blood so bland.
bury the blank paper bodies.
cows with lock jaw embryos,
a private hell in retrograde piano trios,
a broken organ spring that bled.
bury the blank paper bodies."

dizzy

in streets with pee and diseases
i walk with shoes, pants rolled up to the knee,
where liquor stores ran their signs real loud.
guys with gals in jet black & twelve inch boots
got realist drunk;
circle of huffing children in aerosol get false high,
and dance to boomtratic e-box skeet funk.

quarter inch cell of dirty reversal in vinyl ep's,
stolen from stores by pre-fixed prisoners -
jumped free from walls sixty-five ft. high.
those leonard barbed-wire fences bought just in time,
for lines of inmates and disposable rhymes.

a madman filled with grace and pressure -
a youth without the limits measures;
starts his verses and ballistic curses
rage and menstrual pages of lyrics -
poetic justice - a court in bias klaxons of racist.

minds of unstable rap artist of chrome martyrs,
reinventing mixolydian death row rapeivist baroque-folk song.
re-recorded maddening narratives of explicit background -
hard core legends in *128-bit 96.48 surround*™,
"you'll be back when it's di-poligitally remastered,
singed in blood and cum, 24k gold anniversary edition we run."

teenage wizards wait in drones in front of the prison,
waving their privates and pissing.

the *murapeurder's* skull is sloft off with blades in trapezoid
sharpness

his crew wants reparations for a justly death.

record sales scale profit to madness.

a thousand and one cadillacs roamed along -
angry youths left in despondent wreck.

strolled out alone, in two hundred and fifty groups of four,
sat drinking codeine while puffing products laced with gel.
strait dope in winter jackets fully aligned in a city carousel;
strategically placed each notch like a funeral chess board.

the song played loudly on the ethnic gangster bass car -
reading *ebony* with his hand made ivory.
an executed artist has his head toyed high towards a b&w sky.
a thousand more give respect to the recorded memory.

rivers of malt liquor streamed and formed a profound bay.
kids threw *beats* headphones out in the lake like broken toys.
I glanced down at my attire, appeared a homeless tramp,
asked myself, "where the fuck is their money coming from?"

crowds in mayhem slow to a stop -

the vibrations are low, although the song ended – e♭ major -

nothing like the thought to destroy my sex drive.
a drive on the sidewalks in color glass fiber, blunt rolled
loosely - saturday night fires on the streets to ramada dr.

feelings never stay the same if your home is a ditch
if the frame is a bitch inside a canned urine cake.
it's never the same twice if your love
is in multicolored piss streams.
if your pubic lice runs to her as she screams,
into your ear, and out the heart goes!
impossible junkie with three foot heroin hair
trading pills for decent underwear.
its a christmas spent well,
for that the rest of city life is living hell.

decompression's in digital day dreams

Fuck the fragments made in millions.
Too much to count for less time spent.
Arrest the captured again and frolic it.
Sustaining moans kept secrets.
Richly reverberated halls capture sounds,
and evaporates elicit echoes;
like bells ringing in dark equalized formats
of DOS and pre dawn Macs of a prehistoric California.

----- "Only in my dreams was I able to begin in black in white
by trees and familiar factors that lay close to my home.
Only then can I decide to dive into concrete,
and swim in the now colorized pixels of liquid plasma.
Strait into its soft,
warm wet fluids in high def pollutants;
drowning by choice in falsely deciphered vector points.
Muted music gently reach the compressed drum of each ear.
Coming close in synchronization of every 23rd turn
of programmed practical machine gears.
Along with my last human heart beats in this never ending
dream." -----

I awoke.
Embarrassments evoked as my head rose from my bed -
attached on my forehead a floppy disc.
Outdated by standards in Yen and common sense.
I had a nightmare that all my floppys got wiped out by an
industrial sized magnet - along with it -
my old cars micro-cassettes.
Was screaming and kicking magnetic roots by its nest.
A collection like mine can only come from being obsessed.

powder your nose with crushed pills

I'm taking pills on the pillow after losing teeth -
spilling yesterdays Clorox bleach on brittle white hair.
Stares look down at you as if split equally impaired.
Do a line of gold to balance your brain - boost your bread.
A daily space med. Ions charge with static.
Break your body - it's fantastic.

Ted Bundy type jumped from jail last night full of little
stagnant depositories.
The one inside; he's a depressive recessive devoted freak.
The impressive one whom seeks and destroys
people he thinks are whores and weak.
He's the boy who changes your future for the worst in principle
and degree.
He drills on excess, shaved stardust,
in bi-polar remorseful plangency.
Start to ascend upon these pills, and Zoloft is the king.
Prozac with concrete snow skin cased riots
as she declared her right as S.S.R.I. Queen.

The pregnancy rate is up.
A violent idiot sex has erupt.
Hey woman, where's your pride? ...
even rectal transponders swallow whole online.
The dizzy diaphragm aches today after rammed by college
co-ed slut slams.

Kids have children without standards,
and I start to hate the future.
But they will laugh when I die as they say,
"Good. It was his fucking time anyway!"

Those young Rx prophets going to school uptown;
tearing down instrumentation tools,

subtracts rooted bias disses;
spread anesthetic philosophies,
revolving a ring of manic phallus' instead.

Teachers drink Kahlua and spill their Danish sleeping pills.
Shit, we were already ruined from yesterday.
The feeling's the same today as any other.

In my face I show new wrinkles to press back out.
"Shhhh!", she says,
"Open your mouth,
stick out the tongue.
Take your pills,
relax,
come."

unbalanced act

He came out with a cock ring screaming in a rage,
"Oh my uncommon law wife,
leave the room for that I'm setting the biggest fire.
Houses will burn, our neighbors will crumble.
All will reek a roasted rubble in cheap plastic flames.
So please leave with the thrift store collectables,
and all those shopping network goods.
Because no one understands me right now - no one relates.
I'm so low. Don't get in my zone -
I'm so dangerously misunderstood."

She's calling the cops with his phone, but his bill is overdue.

He though, "I must be a few points past mad in prescriptions
past." Then ran away as fast as he could.

e v e n i n g

Violet skies overlap a cliché sunset,
gave synthetic brilliance to unbalanced modalities.
All kids locked airtight into their night light rooms as parents
flip a coin to see if sex is what they should do tonight.
That bites, but as I hear, so does she. . . .
Exclusions include what was robbed from us when children,
and this dullness has taken over my wishing well-being.
Slumber younger me, and pleasant dreams.
You twitch to firebug dance-fly themes.

Wake up for school tomorrow -
abuse friends heads with markers till first sun breaks light.
Ask them over to spend the night. Have and to hold.
Freaking more the merrier - be swollen, not debased by guilt,
and promise all will sleep sound and tight to Stravinsky's fiery
appetite.
Every Boy A#nd F#eisty Girl A#dore D#evising Gas F#ires

65

Bad kids take after their charming parents,
messing with pipes and strike-anywhere-matches.
Rooms pervade still with oxidant supply and
overturned liquid based gas like new farts derived,
but there is no mistake to be found in the simple.
This is toxic, and tiny spaces are filled
with death drowning dreams,
and it seems to habitat it's own area for comfort.

A fire ran fast, cleaning house in a rolling glow of liquid
pristine arms that caught all aflame,
wasted in lame puddles of extreme moisture.
Sad, hateful photos taken for insurance claims.

It's all gone.

Your possessions of unified wardrobes, watches, whiskey and
wheat - sweats the lampblack, trimmed to seared down dirty.

Plastic melted down in retarded shapes,
some twisted in muscular dystrophy.
Memories in wood chard down to younger years,
cracking its last holler of evolved history.
Everything warped from trapped fire looks
pathologically unhealthy and mean.
Mutant sludge of ashy unclean.

It's not what you've asked for; calling you *crazymatch* and
arsonist. Every other fuckup you're locked up with has a
serious problem. Butting heads and fist slamming fights almost
every night is your new creative life. One early breakfast with a
butter knife, you killed another kid – stabbed him in the throat
because he said there are no explosions in space. Every soul
had left before the slightly sane madness began to spread as
fast as their fire stared. Got six aces on top of his sentence, but
never once did that little bastard cry in his cell.

Zions Triangle

My mouth is a trap open or shut. So much had happened since we've last seen each other, but I could barely keep an interest with my past. Every hour feels like our very last. Closed eyes went to sleep, and dream of empty rooms with rope around its rafters. Loosing control – No, I'm feeling fine. Too confused to confess in the nest of low temperature. It may all just be some horrid test I'm forced into. "You take these thoughts with you to Greenwood." They soak in the soil to kill another tree – it lasts long after you're dead and gone. Can't you just let that be; quiet with more mystery in his songs? When leaving the subjective streets, don't look back from fright. You start to feel fractious out from heavy woods; go on without hesitations understood, but the day just keeps on raining a freeze of tiny sharp pains. Everyone wants to find what's more hidden, so the dirt gets marked up like a popular spot of one unknown. Little Zion has its secrets hidden under heavy grounded roots as the rain keeps motion. If you leave a footprint, you sequester your troubles as long as you remember not to stay behind. What is mine I offer yours today. The blues are my body and you've read what is my mind. Here we find ourselves in a closing book of fascinatingly exaggerated times.

The grass was cut clean just before church was turned on Sunday. A barren stem of flat stones, of which just one unknown. *She* says he lays in close with broken vessels. Each ovum carried the seeds of the devil, and the plant holds tight on your cheap wooden casket; asking forgiveness in false pretense. We walked closer towards the certainty of the center - asked our own favors at once. A church can't roll up in flames if evil protects it. So be it. The land too soft and wet to stand long without rooting yourself a trap. Families, Enter on these grounds. All have been subject to choice. Some led away from a promise in prophecy. A simple stance on these rustic stones hold me closer from my own towards god, but curiosity frolics unkindred. To play the vapours touch the crossroads further away, but keep from advertisements - 61 will bite you in the ass one day. Stay in the green – never stray. Ask and leave, for one day you will find. We left behind ashes from cigarettes and took a centered lined exit. Taking time for another - didn't feel anything there anyway.

The neighborhood was in a slow state of decay, and along we followed out from cracked pavements of segregated streets by the open north field. This is where I felt a notorious presence all along my seated feet through a bottom trembling of the Cadillac. Rain still fell, and its drops poured hard bringing the smell of his bones in rushes of mortified chilled humidity and humility. He smelt of cremated coffee, fermented honey in a jar of burnt rosewood. What does a cyanide stricken death spit its odor like? We both walked out a safe distance from the bitter cold cemetery; touched the mud and shook hands in poisoned drainage digging its way in, flashing tense illusioned hallucinations in November presence. Curving notes on along the trail under the eastern covering of the oak, led to the stone that lay his signature. The depression of hundreds of miles didn't deplete nor diminish in strength. But there laid tried bones of a tired man - between trials of an African. ... made his peace with the devil and conferred with curiosity to gods 27. There was only rain heard rolling to– surrounded by announced stones in odd spaces. Don't loose your ground as an earthquake hits your nervous system. Don't fight it, but don't take it. Leave it alone in the dust of dirt. The wooden coffin at Zion, rotting away from the inside takes time for masters and their piece to make strait nines. A train, far away a geodesic line from point a to b, it whispers truth in between. It strains your strongest bases to leave deep wrinkles in young faces.

because we're broken

Desire for empty attention lays grounded -
buried deep in a flower garden
by ways of bleeding fingers
and dirt trapped under nails.
From the bed of newly planted seeds
came an uncomfortable sound.
What was I suppose to caution in your direction
when those dreams and anomalous voices
tell you what to do in that silly head?
It should be examined,
but we get what we pay for. (I guess)
Each of my neurons in the test
reacted like Tesla coils when rampant,
and un-compressed.

This is now my severe panicking point I must confess.

It was Wednesday at midnight by bachelor bypass express,
where I took my cousin Ted to look for his favorite transvestite:
Dominee.

We found him by the corner talking to Clay the Gay as the
other tricks drifted apart in a pattern of equal distance.
It's a dance goodbye when new customers arrive.
They went crazy in the street,
attracting attention by the honking cars
that go opposite ways when finally they meet.
My cousin was high as a kite and getting head outside.
Looker bys screamed and shouted
vulgar encouragements
until the cops came by,
and arrested her and Ted.
I tried to talk the police into letting them go,
but arrested me instead.

Jail cells are roach motels
without the comfortable cushy killing by the feet.
Sweaty men sit and reek of alcohol and dirty fights,
but all found energy when they saw
the attractive Dominee that night.
He turned down perverted proposals one by one,
and Ted took swings at jealous male hookers
that bite after sucking their thumbs.
The room moved manically
as if filled with angry ants
exposed to death metal marches,
and mad cow disease.
Mad men raged with testosterone from an added third testicle,
wanting to rape all that is possible.
Fist went rapidly in random order
knocking teeth around our box of blood spatter
during an anger macho test;
revolved around the beloved transvest: Dominee -
whom smudged and smeared his make up
during facial fractures that persisted.

Is this being severely wasted?
I don't know,
but I think we all may be Charlies bitches.
How broke can I go?
Probably somewhere in between the ditches,
and my parents home.

I went into the colorful city with $2 bills in my pocket.
The change with it was spent on a Metro bus fare.
The two double bills I got from a scrap metal place.
Had a funny commercial on TV ...
a guy and his daughter holding 2 dollar bills in excitement!
The girl, sweaty with tears - a mans greedy face frothing beer;
standing there, shaking their clutched fistful of bank rejectors.
Was sometime early September? I don't know.

Sat in the back -
"got off" before getting off the bus.
Left a sticky puddle in the next seat.
Been about a week.
Lost my cool when I slipped on my own mess,
but took the closest exit left.

Stood on the corner in the wrong part of town.
I stuck out like an extendable thumb.
Should have been watching the stops instead of that
girls boobs bouncing when the vehicle's shocks
smoothly elevated each turn around the blocks.
I tried hiding in the daylight behind a pair of sunglasses.
Still felt naked – bare.
No, of course it didn't stop the stares.
It's not like I was suddenly in the million man march,
but it didn't seem to make a difference either way.

It was the good part of the city.
It still had some standing buildings,
mainly liquor stores in sight.

Man came up with a knife -
said his family's hungry,
"You know; me, my kids and pregnant wife."
Took out the bill from my pocket and asked,
"You have change for a two?"
"What?!?", he yelled.
"Are you a fucking Jew?",
and ran off with the last of my money.

Micro Veggie-table

Notebook of tiny crystals. I've scraped your wood enough.
There's more recycled paper than THC content in this last
formal vessel.
As if you cared when the lighter flicks and the flame hits mixed
chemicals in thick molasses smoke - dithering in your dusty
lungs.
Micro isotopes in the negative tons sweep in blood vessels that
were once tied up - now open to engulf natural poisons -
overflowed with subtle pressure into the beautiful neck.

A small smile to a stenciled look.
You know it's going to be awhile.
Your green is gone - bank account lost hope - waiting for a
miracle before you start off with daily mistakes.
By tomorrow I'll scrape the tube with a greasy Exacto knife -
pretend all is alright.
May even make a mess of this page when I'm done with all the
dirtiness; looking at the deep resin stains,
wishing it was inside me,
taking me to a vicinity I'd rather be ...

Veggie-table land,

with vivid colored happy kitty hands.
Mozart laughs when chasing Calicos' around the bank of
the Rhine.
Chopin in arms with George Sands who gives the most lovely
modern sigh.
Liszt is on a small hill that sprouts opium trees -
rolling around laughing at the jokes Nancarrow brings while
Paganini takes vulgar dry humping to a new level for all to see!
Bach talks poly-phonics with Rachmaninoff as they compare
sizes of their gifted hands and penis.
In the corner by the fence I smoke tea with John Cage to see
who can be the most silent during quiet movements before
Beethoven's fits of rage came swinging abroad when seeing a
flirtatious married broad.
With Clara I run hand in hand in tall summer grass by an
absent railroad track that moves from Vienna, Paris,
and Houston.
Haydn showed up late as usual. He runs off schedule .
In Texas he never gets used to them.

Mozart came running back with a thousand cats;
each with rats hanging from their happy kitty mouths.
The Cat Opera begins with the squeals of rodents when
applying pressure with their jaws.
It was presented at the fancy Warsaw Kitty Opera Hall.
Each act causing the aroused to stand with new imaginations
to the eyes.

But then,

I snap out of Veggie-table land - look at the micro through
large convex lenses, and a geeky head lamp that never quits.
I pack my last pathetic dish, and try not to think if I never get
more, I might just ...

i lost a fillion dollar$$$

Dip your dick between bruises on the lips.
Sacrifice the lamb for protection, for that George Bush is
Uncle Sam with a nuclear erection.
He wants to run as your uncle tom with
no mercy nor compromise.
I've dealt a million hands before I get slouched.
Until Ouch!
A starving family must have taken a bite out
of my saggy ass.

Kill Bill - beating billy -
billion thrills that fit the shitty.
Raised much hell in the middle of
Kansas before deported to Texas.
Got one hundred lashes on stubborn muscles;
it really was nothing special.

We killed pets underwater for Lucifer's father.
He ordered us to build metropolis cities in exchange for
sex with his ten thousand decrepit daughters.
But drowning southern people in the gulf -
Gee Wally, god's really pissed off!

Katrina rhymes with Petrina.
This makes my friends laugh.
I give a lunch dinner to the needy, but hell,
I'm a habitual sinner as well -
my character abstract, obtuse, and seedy.

Went to help out families,
but was caught buying one to take home.
When found out, got abandoned as well,
and left alone.

We're spreading disease in cities while planting carnivorous
flowers *bi*-coastal shores,
eating insectual flesh before rotting hits the meat.
Smell that?
Breath it in deep during medicated sleep.
Damn you're dizzy and spinning around in
sick circles of vomit.
Perhaps you should take another breath, lay down.

Disaster runs deep in the new decade,
disguised as impending wind from moisture
under cyclonic forms of her feet.
They gather like wings of the angry butterfly.
It makes her spread the legs until warm water latched in hooks
to turbulent heads.

Deal with the devil in a game of price as a
lifetime showbiz honkey.
Living in the Astrodome Rape-can of shame -
it's the same since Astroworld stock was risin'.
A million homeless by way of nature cost us plenty in the city
of rap labels and poetic pranks.
So we lost this one, and never found sane mothers again.

casting couch

i sweat too easily because i work too hard.
im a guy who will be a star in the sky over the city
apart in time from consistent sun.
my head is spinning out of text
as vomit rolls down the neck.
mr. blank fills in my spots,
and something in the wind is wrapped with toxins.

im silly - stuck in pretty, and sold a *thing or two*
for hash, rx, dandyridge cigarettes -
on the stony streets i puff to only ash.
from concrete a freaky viscmus approached
like some night crawling subway roach,
and i felt the need to explain him.

the dirty dowager was a pisshole-bandit.
we went to the bathroom to brush his teeth -
an avid french passive worked till entirely beat.
the over-ripe fruit is laughing until turned sweet;
we love random acts / advertised on noisy streets.
some raggedy androids to sort out of the meat house;
watch out for clip queens and the church mouse.
knight of gusset, revelator of the explicit;
now i tire of this game,
different all the same.
the all night looking lounge -
taking in the garbage hand of leftover defectuals.

honking cars go pushy by the show and im relieved
cause i just got blown the morning of this parade.
gave the trick nic-kitty instead of a calming beat.
i feel the need again to pray under stars around me
to keep the peace, and surrender my broken loyalty.

they will lecture when you leave, saying,
"indecisive freak,
hungry little advocate -
fuck me - suck me
wreck me please -
brutal sex on hands and knees."

i sing & sigh, and i laugh & i dance, and pretend to cry,
cause i know im so alright and set
in this endless hollywood screen test.

Vainland

Familiar days - record rooms with spinning needles,
running wax grooves, and the people sank in opaque solder
through alleged clogged sinks - give me my water.
In separation cities, burning down the south -
then the west came fighting,
and that's how L.A. lost its bout.
With the smog and mayhem stranded with loathing pity,
our druggies had lost sight of being pretty.

There's nowhere to drown when all is concrete.
To feel the same as always in this never ending beat.
Busy people cross my path through city declension;
concrete trees smell summertime coming;
flower, pollen, busy bees.
If my time was a savage parade,
I could see through any mess.

In Masonic dance halls of wreaths with ten pound teeth,
I confessed lines of coke with fallen stars of daytime soaps.
Follow the neon signs and triple X feature.
Male gay hustlers are such creatures.
Once even spotted a preacher in white,
using Sunday as an excuse to see 8mm erotic sights.
A few lesbians strapped in leather,
but girls with thigh highs I like better.

Today I woke to the same day as yesterday
because the record player broke 10 times before.
I'm sick of all the things offered me,
because they are few to none.
Still, with all of that said,
any day I'll take my chances then being dead.

Lil' Subversive Swiss Miss (The Swiss Miss Slayings)

History of eaten chocolate crumbs dwell from a past
living hell in family degeneration with inbred
lovers conceiving vampire psychos.
Child killers and pederast breed charming faces that
smile with porcelain hands in hurtful places.
Ringing dirty collars in regret without a princess's consent.

Deep on Swiss mountains that smell of powdered cocoa;
kids and tiny kittens mine for chocolate on a wage of slavery.
The price sky rockets when a miner falls to their death,
and when the family can't afford to pay a funeral debt.

Instead a lifeless body joins other victims of sweet
consumption - rotting away in common place,
where no ones allowed to pray without presumption.
Then pray that she be murdered and replaced.
The child princess with Swiss bank accounts takes the
chocolate crown from her emperor;

after he laid dead from an acute case of severed head.

Her pretty face decorated with lace was
framed by golden twist of braided hair.
A perfectly molded mouth and bright eyed fair.
She smiled with embrace, hiding behind forced haste that was
brought upon by genetics fate inside a devious brain.

The new Mistress of Sugar; divided by power and plans began
to steal children while warm in bed -
breaking families and causing havoc.
The locals now fear and panic
while their eyes are red to wild.

Yet no one suspects "The Golden Child."

Kiss my Swiss Miss Pissings.
Unfair flat rains are dismal boredems out to rein.
Akin to recreational anthroid pox,
spread in high-greek harems.

A miss-carriage concert took stage;
a private play nearly every night.
Lowest basements from a gold granite / level the sky a foot
above bunk beds that recede all breath.
She forced in a cure for ill anxieties -
the strong inhale to windblown lungs infused lining within
powdered sugar & glass.
Her stables shard away between a time the young go missing,
to old age rot.

1693 was the year of missing kids and little kittens as stories
about a cruel woman ran from mouths of angry mothers;
armed with sharpened brooms - ear to ear chanting,
"No mercy for that Satan's here."

A face cake of mercury strikes; cold dead stare,
maleficencly awkward eyes, decisive yet distraught.

It was not the work of the devil by hand,
only from voices heard that presented her with
poisoned lips and a virulent kiss.
We have come to know and love her.
The one we call Swiss Miss.

plastic freaks

Vandergo accidentally shot Lucite,
and turned into a bodyworlds display.
Museum tried to take his cheapened tissues.
I said, "No way Jose."
Buried poor Vander*veins* into a deep earthly crevasse -
a cut-away view of local history.
Funnel-caked his last move – his fluids rested,
then we set Mr. Peanut brittle with private prayers.
A proven love, for the most reckless fool I had ever met.

He had a hyperbolic history of fume abuse.
His sense of smell, as curious to unique in a future chemistry
under kitchen sinks.

Started with a big black marker at ten.
Stole it from school where he learned about
hydro-nitro-oxygen,
his brain flickering silica events.

At twelve, broke bulbs to inhale a mystic halogen -
made his little nose a mistreated specimen for years to come.
Quickly he found pleasures in cans that hissed a synthetic mist
of vapor friends.
Laughing loudly in states of moronic convulsions caused thin
atmospheres of convoluted stars he tried to catch -
fluttering Venus eye traps routinely scratch diode dust.

Played with bags of plastic army men and farm animals,
but they no longer stood up to his new chemical eccentricity.
Cut off heads, arms, legs, even butt-cheeks.
Made them anew, made them freaks.
Trees of army men joined by the melting of appendages.
American hero in disadvantages,
three heads and horse head cock.

His first hit of plastic sessions filled the room of unnatural
odors, insistent giggling, new obsessions.

. . . .

Vandergo became a connoisseur of cheap aerosol cans -
excess in variant fluidity and strength.
Soon neatly separated the array of hard sanitizers,
ant killer and party bug bombs,
scholarly wood polishers to unrestrained diesel fuel,
though his drive for gasoline hasn't fuel injected yet.

Sweet liquified petroleum gas,
Pyriproxifen he shared with imaginary fleas.
Wondrous wasp, you lose flight from the family *Thrin*.
Silly starked wings, inlaid motions,
a sensuous absorption in Sumithrin blues -
pledge to serve Lambda-Cyhalothrin dues.

Tetramethrin, how I love thine taste.
A fatty diet of D-trans Allethrin keeps balance all day.
Sweet wasteful bedbugs I share a light of Gamma-Cyhalothrin,
a trail to your gin by the old Prallethrin.

A heart-on with oz was his only comfort -
his only fixation.

He sprayed long shots of paint thinner into a dirty sock -
took extended huffs and started to sob,
for that it was the most beautiful touch he had ever felt.
The most marvelous thing he's tried.
-No stop to his cries-

Short death breaths he sings,

"Oh my most beloved Toluene
Dilate bleeding bounds
In petroleum day dreams.

Tolley wad in summer
The sniff queen springs
Sweetest breath of a glad rag sings."

He combated the need for fumes with diaphanous stride.
Anytime it came, found fun and short visionary rides.

Most questions pestered his lifestyle;
simply because he couldn't follow.
He sat and found it hard to comprehend,
that his head may be hollow.
Said bye to his delinquent friends and school.
Sat in his room all day vaping emotions,
revelations, he was a mind sweeping fool.

. . . .

With a Radio Shack tape recorder;
created dopey shows and degrading pop songs.
The *a cappella* moron.
Searched deep in a huffers heart,
where this appetite began,
out came a singing start:

$\begin{smallmatrix}4\\4\end{smallmatrix}$

{"Suicide is not so bad when you think about it twice.
Don't be bad.
My razor blades! in my pocket.
Razor sharp! though the socket.
I stick my fingers! in my butt-hole,

but hey -

it's not that bad.
Now you feel like something special,
and your proudness needs more than just one fist.

How about a horses hoof?

A construction cone?
Shut the fuck up.
Is that all you got?
Open wide and put donations inside.
Are you ready for the funny surprise?}

He longed for All-American fame,
but knew deep down his face looked disastrous,
his talent lame -
had an over all appearance of the sick and insane.
. . . .
"Look at those dark circles turning eyeliner black.
Covers bloodshot eyes, frosted eyelids turning back.
Your nose keeps bleeding the marble snot.
Mucous membranes castrate deeper when hot."
- Hey, fuck you.
You lose some teeth for what you need in life.
Pains plague of a swollen mouth and draining liver,
but the high is lined in peremptory silver.

Started a harder habit, collect the types more toxic.
Started a sniff schedule only *pro-fuck-huffs* could handle.

Woke at noon:

- 12:19 – fiend; unleaded gasoline

- 1:10 – nap time again

- 7:11 - wake up for heaven

- 7:22 – hour of leisure; model glue

- 9:42 – start room for the acetone fume

Vandergo huffed a new heavenly era in acetone.
Thought of future chromes and dialectic phasdoms,
a discursive approach into abdicable sciences.

Ideas rush a race inside his shrinking brain,
pushing a pop to transparent hemidemisemiquavers -
Army of Coo-Coo-Clocks - each with a different song.
Tiny swedes in folky fashion circle under their giant bird.

Each clock hung three heavy testicles with extra tubes.
Reminds him of a time in his childhood.
They looked like chained iron shits when holding those heavy
sinkers - sweating hands reveal great thinkers.

Vander's cartridge went a go.
Membranes in his nose got weaker then corrode.
It came dropping off during an all day contest of acetone.
Over the tub, down in the hole.
Nose gets claimed by a troglodytic troll.
He looked in the mirror,
and eruptions of laughter appeared.
Too lifted to care, he said, "Just makes it easier to get air'ed."

Vandergo, still too young, but not in his prime,
turned on the recorder and tried do one last rhyme.
His speech turned to a sporadic recitative of bathos grind.
Rambumbling words in nonsensical ratios that will not bind.

$$\clubsuit^9_4$$

{"Afrooda ceilin nouwh. Jusa berdana nouwh.
Uhmer diddie, ursam ur nouwh. Urmsha bine ceilin nouwh.
(then came the shouting and hissing)
Nas nas! Sssiii! Uhhns! Ul, uhzu. Uhdu bho-bho nouwh!
Boobee Bahhh hissshhhiii! Hisss! Babah–badha, nouwh!
Ima barbum nouwh. Burmzazer yerdokah nouwh!
Isa ner kneeba nouwh!. Numerdoomero. Assa flingering'ing.
Abadoo-doo doo-vod. Rhict putsa abaldoo nouwh.
Ra nouwh! Da-da nouwh. Rodarobbie robum nouwh."}

delivered to stage left (part 1) calculator land

June 98 in Austin, TX I came back from West Hollywood.
Ike and I were being thrown out for not paying rent, and
housing underage vandals.
Just being loud at 4:00AM during Ikes gasoline huffing brawls
after kicking ample holes in cheap drywall.
When it came to say farewell, the place was destroyed and
unrecognizable.

I first arrived on March 17th of 98.
The month I stayed before going west to kiss sanded pacific
lips went long to a solen -
pre-summer heat was defending quickly.
Chain smoking cigarettes by chimneys on Shoreline Dr. -
a million miles from the closet beach,
and opposite the sunrise.

Arrived at night with a stereo, underwear,
and my Korg Trinity, an amp, guitar,
ATR, aphex twin, NIN: *the downward spiral* ... You know?
TreRznor's nineties child?
A wild life inside my briefcase carried love letters
and all that I treasured.
Things in life I've kept and always meant to remember.
Under lock and key that hung from a chain given to me by my
brother.

In the city of Austin I wasn't misunderstood,
but soon lost my ways of being cool.
I dressed too nice for populations of delinquent rats and
raggedy bums.
Students seemed too average when I faced the clock tower.
Asked someone at random,
"Oh yeah, how many shots did Whitman fire?"

We drove back home from the city to our town of Round Rock;
a graveyard computer heap that smelled of burnt capacitors,
and over loaded CPU's.

"The Kids" came knocking in when we called for drugs.
They carried heavy bags of green –
already high as their pants hung low -
speaking in urban tongues that took awhile to seem sincere.
I programmed beats on the sequencer hearing flanerie freestyle
contest behind me.
Strangers came in confounded at the sights of our frightening
group.
This Texas Trash that you now see.

-- Microdensitometer is an f key to me --

Ike had long black hair with shaved sides,
an unmoving set of pallid blue eyes.
He sported a pentagram around his neck from the Texas devil,
swore it never told him lies.
His heavy chains and ruby rings reflected the light away as
protection for his soul and religious name.
"Yes, of course I play first person shooter games!"

90 degree weather didn't stop the misfit from wearing steel toe
boots along with a black leather coat that protruded the
rudeness by his stance on nature.

He does an industrial disco music dance;
sweating in black fishnet stockings,
kicking eyeliner by the door.
Never caring what neighbors thought at five in the morning,
when dust heads cud the thoughts of sleep,
crushing Effergen pills with a bottle of vodka underneath our
kitchen sink.

Still, from the night I got there I hadn't had much rest -
woke drinking Chopin and his Polish potatoes
all morning with strangers' friends'.
One puked after we smoked his blunt of Mexican weed.
Got that kid Maurice to clean it up for free.
Ike came back home from work in ordinary clothes -
went to the bathroom, came out looking like,
"Jesus Christ, Marilyn Manson."
So much for southern fashion.

I got too messed up by the time the sun aligned in its objective
- subject heading west.
The room got darker and heavy with smoke as "The Kids" took
home made drugs to test.
I said, "I gotta take a shit."
Sat down, but being wasted felt like I was thrown in the shower
where I took a piss.
I awoke in the tub with a hangover at five in the evening.
The water was cold and low and noticed I was only wearing
boxers and chemical boots that went up to the thighs.
Came outside with funny hair - grabbed a bottle of Tylenol, and
said "That'll be all."
Then crawled to my little messy room,
stumbling oddly around a thousand tapes and floppy disk on
the floor.
Got in position - fell to the pillow,
and masturbated myself to sleep like never before.

- - The machines made music, and I ate Ramen in between - -

The table and chair stacked on each other facing the balcony
that hung heavy chains.
I sat down on the empty cardboard Vodka case,
and ate noodles off a box I kept obscene audio tapes in.
After lunch I watched the lightning and rain roll through.

Right after configuring all MIDI devices too,
so I shut them off without saving data,
and made a call to California.
Said, "Goodbye" with a broken heart -
stepped out my cigarette butt on our morbid carpet floor.
Started to shout before another wretched rhythmic knock on
the door.
Today ... I think I'll sulk and ignore this noise.

Ike's head hung low when exiting left from his bedroom that
leaked out the stiffening odor of heavy super glue.
A drum machine around his neck started to glitch without
binary respect; making our moods shift blue.

He laid against the wall with metal tools,
taking the fake drummer apart to decide its fate in stereo.
Cracked black shielding off to expense ratios before all is done,
while wearing my Sony headphones in self defense.
I tried to answer him, but instead the pot made me pass out
while huffing markers from Dell.

When I woke, I went to the kitchen for more Ramen,
and by the burner was the dispensed drum machine running at
255BPM.
It was made a martyr for other boxes
that may bomb rotten, in a early Texas Instruments hell.

delivered to stage left (part 2)
"Oh Maurice, You're not quite a Ravel."

Maurice came in all excited,
for that he's composing a rap opera!
He says, "It's about a pedophile and his younger lover."
Looked at Ike retarded.
"How did he come up with this I wonder?"
"What style opera?", I asked.
Maurice stared at me as if I were talking high German.
"Oh, it's all street wit hard core gats!"
I stared back as if he was a god damned brain surgeon.

Ike replied back,
"I didn't know you were a composer Maurice."
"Oh, I'm not.", he said.
But asked me if I could "do tha beatz?"

He sniffed up some snot.
I thought he was on glue.
Ike ignored the conversation -
turned on his Sega Genesis then
flipped on the tube.

"Maurice, you may have a bit more brain to rot if things go
your way, and that's if the glue doesn't clot blood to your
head.", I said.
"What do you mean?", Maurice wondered.
"What did you say about Ray?"
Ike started to laugh while I was trying to grasp the name -
"Ravel!"
If I said it out loud or not though -
who can tell?

"Why don't you do the opera in Italian?
That will make them think!"

Maurice looks dumb down to his Nike feet.
Then comes from his mouth, "Fuck Yeah G!
That would be sweet!
They b callin' me MC Stalin!"

"That's the Soviet Union, Maurice the dumb penis!"
Ike pronounced loudly, "Go ahead tell him Allen!"
I said, "Yeah, you're thinking' Mussolini."
Then Maurice asked comfortably numb,
"Like the Italian stallion Allen?",
Silently thought, "At least he tries."

He then made a heavy Mexican blunt.
We smoked and joked a lot, drinking Coke and rum.
Then I started to stupidly think of his opera. . . .
"Would it work for the public?
Eh, not really. But perhaps for some."

teenage arson trading cards

Me and the little round bastard walked down under the bridge.
We talked about our anxiety of tomorrow.
By the morning we will be in the 6ᵗʰ grade,
but Craven could only talk about the summer we had.
I had my first french kiss, and another teen heart break on the way.
Craven recollected the moments his mom knocked out his old man with one swing.
He laughed afterwords then didn't say a damn thing.

It was a hot afternoon in the big shade.
Listening to the cars go over the bumps real loud.
Looked to my side – not even a single cloud in the sky.
My pudgy friend asked if I was scared about going back to school.
I shrugged it off.
Though I couldn't stop thinking of the bullies that will be back from last year,
and new unknown faces I'll hide from soon.

"Hey look! I found a heroin spoon!", shouted Craven.
"Put that away!" I said, "That's disgusting."
Little pudgy wasn't listening and stumbled upon a syringe.
"And here's the needle!",
Craven said with excremental excitement.
All I saw was disease,
and how much the junkie may have spent.
"Pick it up. Maybe you'll get AIDS?", I wondered.
Craven dropped the syringe to the ground where it cracked in deposit pieces.
"Nahhh.", he said.
"It'll never happen."

I stood up.

Enough of the small talk.
It's giving me a headache.

After all, we didn't go under neighborhood bridges to share our
feelings like two old dykes.
We went there to set fires as we had done all summer long.
It was a way of dealing with boredom as heat made us dumber
with pride, and a shortened temporal telepathy between us
made foul mouths tired while getting ready to start a fire.

Burning plastic baskets made marvelous modern art.
Yet they call us an uncultured generation in this lousy local
environment.
How dare you!
Look at us!
Give me a camera and send the roll of film to NY.
Our bonfire structure is a balanced act installation piece for
private eyes only.

We laid yellow plastic down on tilted cement surfaces that
meet potent ditch water below - linked to lead poisoning,
and why so many localized kids came out slow.
Tadpoles swarm comfortably in the gray tint of standing water
that retarded the green mold of algae.
It smelled like rotten lemons and rusting metal.
A fucking mosquitoes breeding nest.
Time to light the flame.
It should do the rest.

After telepathy weakened down to a Saturday morning cartoon,
frames of our unbalanced act rushed our hearts intense attack.
Each crate we filled with anything laying around.
Mostly long dead grass that buried empty 6 packs of glass.
Newspapers read by greasy hobo hands still ill.
Time must have stood still.

I don't remember all the hard wok of filling 4 plastic baskets.
It must of happened while having fun instead.

Craven took out free matches supplied from Stop N' Steal.
He lit the whole book of redheads and placed it under her ass.
Didn't take long for all the dead grass to catch blond to brunette
in between her unstoppable yellow pubic hair blowing black
puffy layers.
She started to stink that comfortable chemical smell we got
addicted to over the last three months.
The plastic structure started to slowly lean over as if she was
going to puke.

Puddles of flames dripped by her feet.
Quickly going out on the cooler cement.
At the top of her head
hair grew close up to the curve of an echo ceiling.
She was quickly turning
into melted yellow smiles of black smoke.
She shrank, she collapsed, even choked.
She was dying, but we still laughed.
Though it didn't last.

Just by his black shoes and neatly pressed starched pants
you could tell it was law by the stiff rigid way he walked down.
As soon as that tucked in blue shirt with gun locked to my
enlarging pupils I knew to run, and as fast as possible.
That loud alarm went off in my chest.
Just under heart attack mode if I remember correctly.

On the beat of my heart I took a start,
like lap racing around a track.
Started to laugh wildly in the style of jack asses set free.
Then I noticed Craven wasn't following me.
Put my arms up like "What the fuck?"
I looked like a dumb jerk; said, "I give up.",

while Craven appeared from my distance,
a Jesus Christ type with a new disciple -
my triadic vision a mirage.

I got back during mid-discussion,
cop was asking about his dads decision.
A baseball trading card was all his attention.
Had that look in his eyes like he was hard -
You couldn't have missed it.

His wiener and wallet were on Mickey Mantle.
I only had thoughts of being under a judges panel,
perhaps a week at juvenile detention –
come out a re-trained firebug free from sin.

The officer pulls up his pants like Mr. Furley then said,
"I know you start school tomorrow.
You're just pissed and bored."
My tensions went low out my back door.
The nervous gas pushed and soared.

He left us, said, "Good day boys, go home and play with toys."
Craven told me I looked dumb running alone down the ditch.
I looked down at the ground feeling like a real ass and said,
"Whatever Mickey Mantle's bitch."

a Strange life

im scratching crosses in your tombstone,
cause god forgot to give you a home
im loosing peace of mind in this silly head,
taking unjust measures for the dead
nobody would save you when alive -
all my trying quickly died

the drug you chose made life hell
a road from heaven made this short journey the longest tale
you lived with a dog that loved you when everyone else around
you ... dropped like flies
funny i suppose when it comes to surprise,
that you were never really alone from the start
state to state driving from a past you said never should have
been, but that bottle youre holding aint cutting it
that crack in your head wont do,
but you say its medicine for a broken heart
when in reality the last girl you loved,
wouldn't give it back,
and ran far away from you

you wrote a thousand ballads
i could never understand or relate to,
because ive never felt love as much as you do

its the strangest life indeed
call me insensitive to nature,
and disaster waiting to happen,
but when you died -
my life stopped the music you and i began

the parasitic apartment dweller

. . . .Just scared out of my own prepared consciousness. Absolute anxiety held darkness and a hatred of newly curved nervousness with a rope at its thyroid. It forced each into a frenzied rape that gave instant to newborns accumulating faster than drugs can hold a single synapse. It's a fever of a-sexual monomania. Spreading-paralyzing-eating.

Reproduce by fucking oneself internally, then repeat events.

:its brighter outside:

I knelt down in the public shitting position, tightly forced against the corner of the patio by the sliver of open space to peek out on the tiny gated community of Dratbored living.

It made me increasingly nervous seeing the day so bright.

Couples walked - talking of fighting later. Young paper thin moms take their fatherless kids to the pool in plain sight.
Fat owners walk their obese dogs out on poop and pee runs. I closed my eyes afraid that someone may see my half subverted bloodshot eyes surveying back.
Took my head down and crushed inside myself thinking I was the pervert.
I quickly put my penis back inside my damp dress pants. Hell, all I wanted was to take a few drags while seizing a piss – staring down the situation outside.

"Move along."...

I was done, and so was my mind.
The hensa I smoked to "try and deal" wasn't mixing well with retained married molecules; mostly Paxil pissed onto my own claimed bush that I urinate on a weekly basis.
The plant is no longer depressed.
Now I have the animals attention, my cats get stressed.

I did not move until the pain of my inward hysteria clenched my chest, heart, and anus through irregular rhythms;
7/4, 9/16, 5/8, 6/2 - my butt-hole was begging to take a shit real soon.
Yet legs refused a direct order until my rectum came close to failure.

Little loose shots of hot black mold collectively insecure; humidified through gray shades of dress pants.
It crawled quickly with no loss of temperature into nostrils that exhausted waste from lungs we ask to designate.

I looked around once more at the bacterium plaqued patio.
Dried out globs of lung loochers hang off uneven rows of lead painted plywood in states of tubercular crystallized displays.

The floor was too much to think about.
It looked as if a small scale city was razed with opulent hydrogen flames of a fall.
I once lived there …
lowest point on ashes;
under cracks of unelevated cigarette butt ranges.
I crawled out growing freakishly lanky from radiation.
A waterlogged body in castrations which movements made.

Evolved; crawled out of myself to think,
"I'm a museum of my own to wreck."

A girls best friend

Once was a girl of 12.
An only child and quite bright.
She had no friends to play with her.
No brother or sisters to bite.
Played with a red ball, and it ran away.
Caused her to think evil things.
Like to curse her parents during prayer,
and God was a bully that took pets lives,
told the souls to stay behind. To beware!
Either way those days of alienation took a hold to do
its damage on the brain.
Still, she questioned religion, life, death,
if she was even sane,
but these pains grabbed and knotted
her stomach twice in a fight back.
Caused the kid a complex of a full time
hypochondriac.
Lessons be dealt! Values be learned by guest.
Taking the time to think it all through,
because that's all you have when
nobody wants to play with you.

She behaved by the time she turned 13;
Hopped up on good old fashion Ritalin.
Her studies excelled and praised by the best.
Yet with moderate success her peers still pointed
and laughed, causing more stress like all the rest before;
when alone at the park, caught in the dark, dancing and
singing Joy Divisions' Transmission on a short wave all
night long.

Now when she walks in those over crowded halls at
school, some chanted that she was wicked and strange.

Yeah, those kids think they are cool, but keep it up.
You just wait. We'll see who gets the automatic rule.
She started to stay inside her room for hours on end
as any rejected kid would. She read volumes of
biology books as she would lay in bed;
picking her nose where full grown boogers grow,
to create a collection that had no end.

Now a pastime that's become a favorite and quite frantic;
she savors the consistency with a finger and tongue -
sticks them in a ball with the rest under her bed,
when used up and done.

The booger grew 6 feet tall,
into a Greek god of rock hard mucous.
A drying golem stood in front,
demanding the wax in her ears
to keep his movements fluid and greasy.

He smelt of 100 year old dying chocolate that burnt in
war-time fires - came back as rare cheese,
but watch what you say boy!
It doesn't take much to upset the booger man,
all he wants to do is kill your friends -
make your enemies into new toys.
He plays with the body til the fun's over and bored.
He'll twist your little head off with a single jerk;
rip your limbs apart, or just snap your bones -
make it really hurt.
He's your protection in need from those mean bullies and lunch
money thieves.
He harms whom you wish it upon,
then tucks you in at night with a Christmas Eve sing-along.

Even in August.

Yet not all is paradise from your nostrils.
A wreckage of ill wills it enrages.
He anticipates weakness and starts calculating your fall.
Forces you to sit on shitty toilet seats in public bathroom stalls.
Teaches you a lexicon of profanity,
some doesn't make sense at all,
just adverbs of insanity.
Next thing you know,
you're under stress control when dust hits the nose.
Says, "You're a bad girl, don't be sad about it.
Go to your parents room and steal mom's rings.
Smoke her cigarettes and vandalize things."

You thick mutant bastard.
Closer to human, bleeding my classmates blood.
Yet the only emotion surfaced was rage,
but doubt any cage could ever hold you in.
I'll call you Bobby, the last kid that tried to run,
or that cop that tried to stop you in vain,
shooting only a little hand gun.

She tried to believe she had a friend,
but now feared he would be her final end.
Emotions cleared dry sluppy nose digestions.
Slopping her nasal cavity in an empty scooped snot;
unprocessed, moist and slowly warmed to the stomach.

The big old booger man grew taller after endless feedings.
Stankly, fecal odor lines gleamed off his slimy neck;
the center of his being.
A gridlocked tubing running up his heart to the brain;
only way he stayed alive to entertain.
But, she got the fear of his control,
and grabbed her fathers shotgun, kept loading rounds.
"Booger got shot to shit.", til no piece could be found.

boxer blues

When eyes flared on that cute boxy bastard Moxy;
I knew Mami, Sancho, Libby, and me became obsolete
as lifeguard family.
We were rounded up and sectioned off in different parts.
I got dropped off like a wounded animal at a park.
Texted my cat Sancho who got held patio prisoner.
He was reluctant to return the message until he submit,
"This is a trio of horse shit!"
Nothing figurative about that as I got tired breaths
commanding sweat.
I lay lax under a tree texting back, "Go Sancho! Attack!"

paragon fluid draining head – Dayz of *Amplifibility rx*

I arrive pretty late to Bosch's still buzzed from earlier.
Told him about 10, but looked at the monitor; said
"shit", or "fuck", or "whatever".

Took my girls car and watched out for creepy condescending
coppers that hid in shadows with radar beams protracting from
shaky hands that itched to touch their fully erect penis.
After all, some have lousy cheating wives to fuck at home,
but no, they are out having the time of their life as you keep out
of sight from the public's eyes.

You're privately contracted to eventually die by a good chance
in statistical terms of your particular city.
It's a pity I keep rhyming just to make assumptions pretty,
and write of some made up cop whose hands are covered
in dried sperm.

texted: utsride

Bosch opened the door and said,
"Hello! Some fucking heavy speakers fell on my head!"
Asked, "Can you function right now? Are you even well?"
"Yeah, just a concussion with slight blindness and minor
hemorrhaging.", he mumbling said.
"Want some ice cream?", I asked.
"Fuck yes!" Oh he smiled so big and bright.
Then I went to his garage to smoke a cig.
Looked at his crystal diode easy cheese radio.

"Hey, what about that ice cream?", Bosch stared to ask.
I said, "No thanks. Not hungry. I'll pass."
"Well fuck … I have some in the freezer.
You want some I guess?"
"Fuck yeah!", I shouted.

He laughed then asked if I wanted magic shell on that.
"Of course! Make it a double!" I added!
Bosch went in the kitchen as the cherry got hot to my lips on
the little cigarette butt. Smells of low class fiber glass.
The hot orange ember must have fell from the butt and hit his
lap top keyboard while downloading hard-core barely legal
German porn.

Bosch arrived back in the garage with
two bowls of ice cream!
I took one and said, "Thanks. I'll be right back."
Put the bowl of sweet milked titties on top of the toilet;
pulled out my stinky wiener and peed dark yellow.
Zipped up and stared at the mirror;
asked the world, "Ready for more?"

As I came back, Bosch asked if I had brought a hard drive.
"Let me check my grocery bag.", and I threw the bowl of ice
cream in a recycling bin that was filled with Dr. K soda cans,
pounds of ashes and unrolled roached zigzags.
It was last years ashtray of phlegm,
wearing expensive coats of fur -
this seasons next Sotheby's specialized dumpster.
He looked pissed and pointed at me.
"You dick. I just made you that ice cream!"
I said, "I don't need that shit.
This isn't a Weight Watchers dream."

Quick I went out the door without a hug or goodbye;
this is how it feels on Amplify.
I shrugged it off acting sordid.
Seems I've turned mean when awarded ...
the biggest drama queen reported.

mouth to pout

Strait and balanced is how I acted
before we moved in together.
Now that I'm a comfortable wreck around you,
the talk and sex makes us apathetic yet rue.
Today I woke next to your smell, and it was the worst I've felt
since you got me to quit smoking.

Nicotine – farewell my chemical love spell.

The parking lot has a lot of butts this morning,
but I take my time to pick up the ones with the most expensive
tire marks.
I took a deep drag and said, "fuck."
It was the greatest moment in months.
Smoking Mr. Flaty went quickly,
so I looked around in someones patio ashtray and had my pick.
The nicotine hit my nerves,
til I didn't want to kill you with arsenic.
Instead I keyed your car a little in the back
where I sat looking like a full time maniac,
smoking my pocket full of flat-head cigarette butts.

For three minutes I felt a harmony with my surroundings again.
I started to remember when morning joggers didn't piss me off
as I sat on my ass eating a brick of cheese,
and the sounds of early morning machinery didn't drive me
mad to the point of yelling obscenities - foreign workers whom
didn't understand me or my rantings.
A time I didn't want to shoot birds that were frantically non-
stop singing.
No! These three minutes I smiled with the sun,
and may have even waved to driver bys, perhaps two or one.
Yes. It was such a glorious morning instead!

I walked back a different man with a gracious attitude towards
my general existence …
until I saw that fat snoring face of yours.

Snorting and squealing along those fucking 8AM sirens,
landscape machine cutters buzzing with less desirable
decibels in my aggravated head.
When they stopped and silence finally made its entrance,
you farted in the bed and woke up to the smell of
dry mustard flowers dusted with garlic.
A bead of sweat from her butt cheeks dripped to her asshole
and fogged the room with humidity that dogged my lungs with
microscopic fecal matter.

It feels heavy on the chest when I break sweat.
Now my pores drink for the golden musk.
A cup that holds her perspiration from
areas of the skin that are wet and hairy.
Places that have no light.
A place where stink lines are even visible at night.
By the time you rolled out of bed I was already in the shower
cleaning off your sin, when I came back out
you had left for work with a doggy bone in mouth.

The day was turning out to be another shitter.
I rolled three joints and went to the park.
As soon as my ass hits a comfortable spot,
landscapers with the same fucking noise machines
rolled up and down the hills.
The birds got aggravated,
vocalizing their need for complaints.

Soccer moms ran in an early jog, stopping and turning around
when they see me as if I were the local raper.
By now my boiling points told me, "You're still addicted to
cigarettes! Perhaps I should try the vapor."

I sat on a bench for three hours smoking a joint each passing,
and all I could think as I was stoned and finally alone was,
"Yes. I need some nicotine.",
but had combed the park to find shredded butts
by oily blades of baroque Mexican machinery.

The park looked beautiful.
The weather surprisingly wondrous,
but hated every moment as I obsessed on personal poisons
from my past - an empty box of Pall Malls in the trash.
Then at my lowest moment I heard a little squirrel laugh,
demeaned my mood crushed to physically cynical.
This is another unfortunate point and its pinnacle.

I ran faster than I ever had to catch that squirrel.
It was nothing more than pure determination,
knowing that in a short time
I will have committed an abusive crime.
I picked the bastard up as it made personalized marks
with sharpened claws, and squealed loud with insanity.

The combining pain stabilized me.
I didn't think of the evils of nicotine -
setting new rules on just how to relax,
during the signs of major panic attacks.

I put Mr. Squirrels head under my shoe;
slowly stepped down on its fragile skull,
until pressure of a final pop slowed me down
to where I was this early morning,
slow & calm until the next step I do wrong.

My mind – a psycho addict discotheque -
a murdered tie swung proudly from my sweaty neck.
Breathing techniques bring out the crazy in loon,
strolling down the hill, gargling a sailors tune.

head

do everything you are told.
counting down your fingers to the toes.
your crows nesting in silica stance
eating pro-hydrofibre fungus.
we awake with purple mushrooms,
and faith turns a fatal garden gift
to drowning salmon with significance -
upstream to flowers of test tube phallus'.
something deep a garden grows.
smother your skin in grit and dirt;
small broken shells slit under nails - make it hurt.
take down that button up shirt
let the dirtiness feel you again;
letting the mark of your memory drain
to a wishing well as stains set in.

a temptation grows deep,
longer than ever felt.
inside the closet – outside picture frames -
taking buried photos out from the rain.
take in sleep with surrounding pills.
yet don't step close to edges during a dream;
protection in the bowling green of benzedrine.

i wait for the sun to end
then to God i make amends;
for love never closed within the casket,
open for bodies and static -
the spirit in your attic.
emulators cross violating paths
with transmissions never complete.
take it slow – then hesitant to eat.
becoming frail to skinny -

noise effects your station
inside polluted relations.
slowing down your time worn train
before the wreck becomes absolutely profane.

this summer is cold,
and don't disturb the blaze of furnaces;
once tx fields in low grace periods that year.
all this hits you harder when you feel to sink -
standing the direction of the sun and look really hard,
to think and forget what you've become.
no one recognizes you – as vacant as burdensome.

it's ok to keep far away from dogs rabies, ticks, graphic bites,
and heavy unhinged teeth that breath profusely.
train mr. slave well for that he attacks the dog in heat
before it's cut into pieces of ceremonial meat -
a detestable disease buried at unmarked cemeteries -
alone in overgrown masses one cannot carry alone.
still we prey for our enemy's to be show their way
from earths ravage reigns and momentous calamities.
take them all away until the last moon of mornings day.

The Daughters

They told wicked stories of a terrific nature to children
before closing their eyes and going to bed.
Kids now praying patiently to God,
reciting verse in cold sweat after all that was said.
But we remember what we don't know
with extraordinary promise to what may lie ahead.

They come a little closer with half closed eyes,
staring past midnight,
safe enough while heaven watches in false light
that burns my retina.
Not yet blind, it was time I would suffer
for the rest of my life -
never to see colors again,
and only in this spectrum will I dream.

Polarized sights with Rapid Eye Movements in the opaque,
the only thing I survived from my world of gray and blackened
staccato stains.
Is this the dream?

Somewhere close to the woods,
is a land of claviers fallen from the sky.
Smashed boxed frames,
and splitting ivory teeth
play from a perfect roll;
walking past pivoted pianos,
they growl with tampered strings.

The ground wants to rumble,
yet the sound not deep enough to bury.
I can't stand the resonance.
Eh.
It's what the bones in my head despise.

That ringing in middle ears only persist when stuffed with
dissimilar dysentery – time to buzz my teeth in electric shocks
of grinder incisors.
Strange smells that enamel burns.
Quick inhales knocked on new visions;
as fazing hunger starts to unfold.

A trick of modern minds exhumed fresh meat.
Cracking spherical glass that separates the atmosphere from
heaven – away from protection.

The moon springs closer an auditory singularity.
A last love in pragmatic amplifications -
ground getting louder in illuminations.
Corpus of waves gathered smallest currents in deep silence -
breaking stone into shadow – turning loose ripples re-gated,
never to stop its own recycle.

A bird comes with mourning words -
flies away before hundreds of questions must be heard.
Our planet and moon close to crashing by the waning string,
tension reversed in a lonely orbit.
Loudest nine tones an ear can handle;
starts to shake all gravel when they sing.

"Walking the fire", and gravity keeps it grounded -
four to eleven paces in places resounded;
fifteen hundred and six dead zones counted -
fast to reproduce where cultures fade then vanish.

Two dilated moons appear in new space after consuming the
afterbirth in its place;
still producing too much waste in openness.
Trash takes over the world,
and there is nowhere to live.
New daughters born to die from our dirtiest line in lineage.

texasippisaws, Arcanaz

Hop scotch – hillbilly tree,
full of bare branches once decorated by leaves.
The seed has expired like families of the beast;
killed off by southern hospitality during breech of the farm.
An intruding host to the wood as its virus.
Keys and beer bottles hang from these trees -
weathered strings wrapped with wire.
Then a romance begins in dry roots from rain,
but the roots too far to save when we think
of all the damage from the bugs in the soil,
that feed til turmoil is reached when tasted by its
own disease.
Heat moves in white hot light until it's humidity.
Anything colder than what's outside sweats;
diluting ones self.
These objects licked off from bacterious strays;
thirsty for drops left behind.

I'm sad when it gets crowded in
these parts of the dead wood.
It's the season we can't reach a reason for
the horrible things we do.
I say this because I'm guilty as you.

Kicking old tetanus cans till the revelation begins.
We can sit down,
and then enjoy the end with post prejudice eyes.
Those little men in simplistic Satan form shut down the sky
with prehistoric coiled magnets defined towards the equator;
half way from the core and its crust.
Planes of unspecified passengers came balleting down in
circular strides to denote the nominal in phenomenal displays
of power when loosing trust.

The blimp in the sky wants to crush back with strive
from an eccentric aircraft stuck in its side,
but history becomes the hero
to those saved from incline.

Ascrowagg, a flight of ways flown;
never above,
recede and to shove;
Away below a bionyte becomes.

Don't doth the little one we call the guttural itch.
Generation flus of fragile flaws kept in tectonic plates that
varrid.

There is no trouble in Paradise
(if you cannot find one yourself, *2014)*

Watchful prodigal witnesses prevent what was wry until further confess.

If you were born in 77, you lost faith when 11,
now searching for heaven.

If you were born in 79,
a mid-life crisis now show its signs.

If born in 82, got confused when 28,
ran away with your first date.

If born in 84, maybe a career working whore?

Your born in 86,
now in a war, you don't give a fuck about two shits.

Born in 88, you have an intuition the future's not that great.

Received in 90,
drugged before grade school kicking and fighting.

Received in 94, now clinging on legal synthetic drugs,
ones like never before.

Received in 96, when turning 18 you're a hit or miss.

Born in 97, naive and indifferent with error in automation.

Born in 98, you're generational swine with contest of suicides.

Born in 99 into ignorance, profane kids of scientific poetics,
born to die at 26.

F r a c t u a l fictions

Ashes hit and crumble apart on the work desk
when we found chrome based tapes in winding click machines
running the voices of rumored spirits backward in phase
through tiny speakers separated by 4 feet definition.
Sound of collected magnetism unlock cable synchs from fried
electric chords displaying a vulgar ultra-vision by divisions in
schematical variables unknown, but the test have shown
decibels ranging incredibly high by summertime.

Advanced evaporations conducted in samples collected from
the ark of gold that was sold during cold war fears and
90 minute tape loops in her lamentation of sex.
Listen closely, she's reaching for that second to last breath.
She expressed an antagonistic concern of
"man made wars by the foot of the bay."
Until the stranger with a splicer slit her throat
before she had more obscure arrangements said.

"Amen!", be shouted when this world came to a
progressive close; ruining a millenia of ignorance shown.
Her yield was vast in importance when you stay uniform,
but you must close your eyes not to go blind.

The head of a human can bast in the sun for
days before it's inedible.
A brain is useless if hooked up and poisoned by
humane machines when better in the stomach of
a self-proclaimed king.
His value is knowledge until
riddled with madness on her side.
Strings come up inside and posed her stature in
a crushing recoil of fractured knees.
Shelter me, and I will be your slave.
Love me and I'll run far away.

wrongwordswritewell

as the words came strait from my mouth
a dead man writes the book instead
when my life changed to chapter six
i didn't want to ever look ahead
but now this verse is taking its toll
as if i didn't know
my role in life anymore

sing to me but change the song
dance with me before the
circumstance is all wrong
laugh with me but stay very quiet
hate with me before they
reinstate loves riot
then there is empathy

a page turns over towards the south
the dead man in the casket turns his head
as the sky revolves to fire from drought
i found they were cheap plastic roses in his bed
this is the chapter in which im told
that i never really know
what lies for me ahead

sing to me but change the key
dance before they advance
to the nearest sea
laugh with me and arrest the siren
hate with me before we irritate loves tyrant
then there is nothing there

the dead man looked at me
said nothings wrong

i took his hand and went along
his head turned to the north
and sang a song
to find there was no tune at all

reckless wrecking wrath

From the woods it crawled out
greeting the first sign of day.
Breathing fast and found
way through stages unsound.
Sweat standing back in baking
basket caged dumbest designs.

Watch the counting on owners wrist
waiting to converse unisef.
Locks and jaundice looks
from closed corners too dark before bed.
You lay silence in summer nights
to offset symmetrical shadows.

Relax entrapped blistered pre-heat hotter;
realized destiny's proved backstabbing or unsolvable.
It's that insensitive weighted pull,
effecting the cause and hoaxy high tides aligned to xy-39.

That invisible force struts around;
never obeyed us on the ground or in the deep air sky,
where Deuteronomist jury as one embryo justly swayed,
up and down with ring arounds side to side.
A walk too prideful for man,
then again it doesn't access this trait.

Goes in strait lines leaving agnostic carbon traces.
Spread what you said in mystics false pretenses.

The world, if proven flat would aflame the map;
the bottom incinerated before the turn of the sun's elapse.
A gulf is now the pot of oil that sparks a great pulling steak;
unclog the feet in future sales but no, it's still too weak,
calling nature-in-law a freak.

Gimmie
give me
gimee oxygen and stronger wind paths.
It's only scared of dying out in a puff dust delirium.
Closer than human I purpose.

Fear enthralled a move, as to reproduce with non-replaceables,
leaving a generational scar - miles worth the time sun danced
on earth to outshine moons tide.

My shadow left a mark that gets more dark over seasons.
A concessional stain of mono carbon exceeds recent living.
Radiant Fahrenheit without the sun is hotter on the skin,
charring to every center it tastes.

It finds large lands of oil derricks spread to horizons corner.
A clean scorch on sticky sand burns an ocean wider than hell.
An ill-used Megiddo erupts under combustion it exorcizes.
Imagery so perturbing, it would make you arid for life.

Dashes jump to dark dots,
a parallel dimension in Days of Noah.
Death of the sun turning a dense *Novia* bang;
gives the earth away to a silver belt.

Quickest exit north left,
when south right at home,
comes and goes again.
Saved and condoned.
Lost and accused.

veteran resin

Lunatic is a word for the me I used to know,
figured was sane before the battle blew over.

They strapped me in a uniform with
weapons and a suicide pill,
then transported me far away up into the hills.
Said to keep quiet,
threw me a gun and go kill for reasons of peace.
Told me all were enemies that need to be carried to hell,
but I missed Sunday school when I was young –
found it a hard sell.

Why are you boys shooting at me?
I've never called an insult.
I never met your mother -
don't even know a name.
I stayed down in a trench fighting for freedom,
but I signed up to die in unkind lands –
a wide open malaria prison.
It's been hours since a required silence during
machine gunned fire.
Would once in awhile see a man slip in mud
and never get up.
Wet dirt with blood didn't grow flowers,
but eventually bore a cross in your home town on
half empty coffins filled with beer and nails.

That's all I know when you die here.
You get to go home, and forever you'll stay while strangers
wave to kids in a patriotic parade.
It's just down the street from your resting place,
but your ground is depressing.
Sometimes they rather not remember you're dead until the day
they forget about you completely.

I came home a year later without the attire of a body bag.
Didn't lose my arms, chest or legs.
Didn't get shot and left a war with minimal pain.
I looked fine my family said,
and threw me a party for dodging bullets.
They sang, danced, and said a prayer for soldiers who died
while I missed my party to stay in my bed to cry.
Nightmares of killing faceless people rang in my head with
ballistic injury instead as the people outside have the time of
their lives.

I'm a shaken man by our nations side,
waiting for god to let me go to sleep and die.
Post war syndrome is beyond the cocaine in my stomach,
and slowly it's spilling my honey and
grapes that once were sweet.
Yet all I taste is warm metal that oxidized from
the blood of friends.
It's bad the war is over so they can start the tragedy anew,
but I felt a need to be heard as I spit and froth from my mouth
of opiate seeds.
"Remember when the apple trees I planed started to bloom
before I left?"
I was just a child who never thought of the future til now when
it seems too late to try.
My eyes took to novice contemporary life,
and told the young it's all an invective lie.
They shouted back,
"Where's your end of time sign?", and laughed.
Never mind, it was just me betting on dares,
so once more I made an empty prayer.
To who? The blues of Asia?
No. I sat so still and silently by-the-way -
on a old broken veterans lawn chair.

Messenger

It stood there in the silence at my naked window.
Noise and all movement void in the body.
It didn't care to come in as it knew its terror was frightening.
Eyes made sense in delirious nightmares before the sleep.
Too nervous to rest my pupils that whispered instructions
in granite of consumed symbolism.

3AM is the most private hour of Earths cycle,
and reminded to stay inside for that I would die that hour.
When we talked the emotions felt were completely mine.
At the dark behind its head shined absolute black.
Night covered by eyes that took no color at all.

I soon felt a world with blind eyes as our spectrum departed.
Emptiness expended with or without the personality of time,
the only constant clock is the beating of your own heart.
Still waiting in blindness because we are, and we will.

From the start of stares from discussions above,
beware of your thoughts while dreaming in bed.
Next before you know it you're wishing you were dead.

Existence becomes a living hell in your shell of decision.
No way to translate in dangerous thinking of words dwindling;

Right before it came near a diminutive halt.

lover reheater

shadows and casting follow the train that hits me
instant fear holds and tricks by powers above
making bombs in shelters for people
praying to god in a demolished steeple
hold close to what you love dear
save the souls who drown in the after party
cheer - second act is done - stage is on fire -
applause and bullets are what we waited to hear

picked up a grenade from the road
love the feel of steel that was cold
i cracked my head open to feel the blast
nothing can take me - nothing will stop this
save me from bravery - save me from violence
save me from symmetry -
nothing sacred can save me from silence
negligence is nothing - save me to stop myself
nothing now can save your commonwealth

people put up your hands & clap
gods waiting for the encore wrap
dance, drunk, fuck, lets roll
collapse! - didn't have time to sell my soul
a final chorus tells me of another grind
go away with yours and ill take mine
if you feel the uncomfortings' harm then fall in my arms
amplify bright tonight till the last damn cloud
drops from the sky

i sang screaming in a lo-fi microphone
turned a riot into blood and quarter tones
ministers became mad at our sound systems
separated states sink low to take tomorrow with weapons
now all hell breaks loose in the streets far from heaven

before the after accident opaque was the sky
we felt the warning, yet ignored the click-it-ing clock
time again to put on your boots
walk through treacherous miles of bullshit
don't fall on your pride with your face on the ground
no shit – around the world it never ends
until the day you reach your friend
they're not cold or adjusted to temper
a new year not proceeded by winter

let me please sit. let me dry my eyes
under the eclectrostraticphere
i want nothing more than to sing with you,
and live this common surprise

Parade – Post

Insects wound on a strip of tape to alleviate my sympathy
came framed by every hour –
to each second of conceptualized time.
History can't seem to redeem itself from sin, yet that
formidable march still goes on - stomping the city down with
thousands of citizens that embellish their status patriotic.

After the war a friend without his legs came back to
congratulate, throwing tinted flowers at the parade strutting by.
A cousin who lost his arms would sing the anthem song,
then sigh to the brothers lost whom died.
But the hours go by so slowly as songs of rejoice beats into the
brain with its special rapid pace - swinging baton bats and
sprays of hydrochloric mace.
The military police stop and sing along to the fallen song
before a massive crowd of gas masked protesters light
cocktails, stopping and setting dirty bombs.
What the world needs now is hate to create new economic fears
of haste - shown exactly where we've gone wrong.

World leaders are now dominating preachers,
then self proclaimed prophets.
Salvation in blueprints reckons teachers.
We never proved god is dead.
If true they will replace god with a government instead.
No ones calling a state, and the lord's not calling a home.
We reinstate ideas better left dead.

An empribiblical state displays the emperors body
laid in a case for this is the end of a war,
but to begin an opening for a new door.
A modern light on dark revelations; we were shown what we
had lost, and we misspoke from the ancient context that
transcribes events for the future of war.

I feel picky when forced to choose my own cause&effect, made
to worship cliche folklore from our time before.
Evacuations dedicate to static eruptions when channeled
intravenously.

Oversized veins choke-hold arteries; pumping in my mixtured
blood from cheap machines take the feeling
of grievous expansion away.

If the revolution ever ends I'll carry dead maggot meat
on a stick, high as freedom allows in constraining laws.
A new government; the fresh Parish has no ways of repair,
and we sense what is wicked or fair.
Who follows who when all are in the same desperate despair?

There is no more link to the ancient from new;
from the massive to the only few whom knew our histories past
when all turned digital, and erased in single flashes towards a
dwindling dissimulation.

Shame on us!
None to accost the condemned cast that held knowledge!
Duplicity becomes favor despite what the remainders say,
and *kiss the ass* to what was yesterday.

neuter

stop breaking down
no favors with sadness
what the excuses could do
my down is done with throws
for god ran syphilis over a trite
the defects standing there to fight
too much for the weak i impaired
your oral praying of all hellish cells
sticking fingers out banged distance
excess in ears turn lights when asleep
last nights hash of Kaldra in stash mixes
then seeking truth down clouds and traps
suddenly flinging tops of bugs to milk biotics
lapping in my wife – flashing mics in with insecticide

Ay, Bunker Hill,

> The Defects don't fear the south in EXIM evictions.
> We've got detention tickets to the riot-rob,
> but careful with parallel parking jobs.

Now turn down the lights – you've done much abusing.
A weakness in ears when asking god for favors.
Sick ticks of mascara on your first cousins ring.

Stop breaking down

Baroque-folk harpsichord, barbeque chicken prelude and fugue
sandblasted in eighteenth-century Italian yellow and reds.
Off with that cake-faced arsenic head.
Ludes away guillotine ghetto blaster's blade.

Ran syphilitics north her canal.
Unconscious full cousin; don't fear the south.
Don't fear my bug infested mouth.

A wedding orgy under rotted chapel stills.
Standing there on Hunker Bill;
coughing phlegm, spitting blood;
choking on lung, tucked away in uniform.
The circus is borne battle;
bugs tucking under skins.

HMO is my dearest friend.
Take a stand in the final end
because God is judging you.
Make sure to miss the flu this season;
the reason ... you're broke.

s   h   r   i   n   e

Black & White, Red & Blue,
these colors run virgin Mary's womb.
Never tasted her tentative reign,
nor listened to instruction obtained.
You're not a master of your enemies.
Don't waste time pretending with pleads -
it breaks your homeland of tripping lips
that lock to the touch, then disband.

run Mary run
don't lift your head too high
above your roofs - it takes your life
run it, hit it damn you
the machine of life
fixing, pushing,
alternate wishing wells

Tell yourself, "*you have some pride*" -
always a flag in motion, self sustaining like an ocean,
putting your cells in place - take it honey.
Push it somewhere new, and push it in design.
Skyline new obstructions for,
structures relaxing;
structures collapsing.
Push it away from fear, push it close and near.
My minds away for the day.
I leave it with God.
Prayed really fucking hard - let up my head and dance.
Gain high properties, stabilize the insane by chance...
One day it will come so efface your mind.
Say goodbye.
To sin is to live, breaking paths of younger years,
and along came with it, personal wrath.

mad garden meat

Walked hours down the creek hunting for thirsty travelers
Paralyzed them before putting to sleep
Transferred the high off DMT released before one dies

We picked them off in twenty twos, one by one
Then my time arrived
Plummeted, beat with heavy slats
Became an angel, dark on sun's path
My body played with
My mind still dreams of anatomancy myth
An effect I can't concur as brain surgeons exist

They consumed my head raw
Consorting cold kelvins rocked back to sleet
How quickly the trident sleeps in red sickle cells
Thaw the sawed monad meat

Hillbilly high life
their philosophy underdone
The sky was the limit
And past owned a jack of oily resin rags
On a whim

As a whisk of whiskey seeds and stems
Pressure cooking steam with boiling heads on splinter spines
Around the burning rim
Time to search and seek fresh cortex to freeze and store
Kept dead and quiet

My spirit walks as your only friend
Keeping mind when the suns back again
To a place we used to meet
Chigger Creek

A train's coming

Mono magnet meat relinquishes duo-protein cells
when earths field starts a fade.
A finishing touch on reactionary delusions,
magnificent relays rewinding in trident orbits.

Predicted events plague a mans mind full of forward clocks,
even numbers, grinding life against an acidic rusted razor -
checking locks non-stop until all times wasted.

A scorn of averages balance you off the square,
giving freedom to those whom practice calculated havocs –
the same that pray to gems of superstition.

Back handed a gypsy during smoke breaks of battle.
Neither side ran,
so all be damned in wastelands of wreaths and crosses.
Then to ask, who benefits from it?

Neptune concise towards the seven.
Two dots become conscious,
then your head splits in halves,
unequaled in oil, gold, nor Pisces.

Gigadam is linear an empire rises.
Open smile til cracked tire.
Write Joy, Fire, War;
we live through code,
to protect and server.

the 43rd

Right before noon I went to mass today and prayed
with an empty brain. Made a stone of my heart.
Something tells me it's just one of those days
that have frayed - supposedly by a shitty start.
Rear view mirror with a crack in the side,
and the little ticks to destroy my time.

So much integrity - much awkward pain.
I wish it all away,
but today I have something else on my brain,
and I listen to the brass band passing way.
All trumpeters on ground with bloody horns and hands,
are getting laid then die like roaches on their backside.
God knows why,
yet still, one damn thing is on this mind.

The pro-con have the bomb to rectify a war if provoked.
Parades are just a riot with military police,
destroying peace makers at an American square,
as lips kiss my ass on the ground getting my fare share
of stock holders beatings.

A rolling red looks sharp on black pavement
if you can take a hint.
Philosophy of anarchy allows no boundaries in government.
To sink a thousand vessels missed you must first kiss ass
before extinction inks.
But hell no! It's piss from the stream I drink!
I say, my ship will never sink!

Mine is used and abused by few.
I'll never sing the shit out of luck blues.
I have 100 million rabid, vile savages masked into one,
but it's not your loss. It's not a Jesus on a cross.

Don't get carried away by the day of false surprises,
and what your cold heart entices you.

Structure applauded with war,
the greatest fight.
Pre-futurists' bitter atavistic sights -
our biggest fuck-up comes back to bite.

Northern drinking unions came x'ing inspiration,
a $Dollar War$ worth dirt liquor.
Two out battles advises destruction
as deafening testing poisoned us.

naturulistic

½ time made malevolent air pressure dive into an oscillatory
apparition of noises bearing faint assisted tones,
advancing in like another vicious cycle.
This one consumes the malady and becomes it.

No sign,
no word received that it had decided to slow or stop.

The way this spread will halt is if it's aware that it wants to,
it would statistically be like surviving a cyclone;
dead on what's wood, glass, and pestilential nails.
It does not decide it's too dangerous or arrogant,
to stop the repeat.

It doesn't know shit.

It appears deadly and bossy by accord.

Creation.
The nature of progress and program.
The art of repetition acts regardless of who can see, hear, taste,
touch, smell, screw & steal, heal and murder.

It's not your fault nor its host.
This is the nature at awakening.
It's not the fault of machines and their faulty programmers.
Not the fault of a particular government or its people.
Not the fault of virtue nor depravity,
but all lay effects of its duality.

Stop saying stop,
and stop your exchanges to continue vices.
Not your fault. Settle down with your lasciviousness.
Put every person on this delicious earth in chains,

it would not cease to be languid.
It makes no difficulty, nor spares more time to find you.

Tasteless, odorless, despicable, depraved, delightful, effective,
dead-pale, every time never to fail.
Inventive yet static, forming spikes to standing waves.
Erratic, but never dramatic; we would most likely kill ourselves
than become disowned invalids.
Extol our exceptions.
Grace communications abroad.
It is not silence or the whisper absent.
Not the breath of the living cataclysm.
A scent brought on by the living rod.

The universe will engulf its own to solid ice,
because she's known as a freezing cold bitch;
always playing with a pair of zocchihedron dice.

two of me

I am as much good as I am evil;
as giving as I am greedy,
as cursed as I am blessed,
as enlightened as I am perplexed -
God damn I'm a confusing mess.

+ crowds +

There's something telling me what I need to hear.
It's racing through crowds and stops at places
that are noisy and deep.
Electronic noise in the jungle won't break the message
because now they're friends -
waiting till the end when they find me.

This message is something deep I think.
It's natural yet mechanical to uplift my spirits,
and think of me in this time I'm blue.
Like a rock waiting - never shifting -
always standing over you.

It parts from its messengers and
races for its purpose again,
and there's me, no where to be found
when I hide and pretend.

I **shout,** and **scream,**
and **yell,** and **pound** my feet onto the **ground,**
and then I stop and listen - still no sound.
"W*hat's taking so long? I'm anxious and tired.*"
Should I just jump in the water
so my thoughts won't catch fire?

Perhaps it's just me - a delusion in simple solutions
caught by the other me.
I'm *schizoid* - an absolute *frenic.*
Never wrong when I tell my savior he's right
as I fear the day will come;
when I finally have to face the insight,
and act as if I'm actually sincere.

displays *on* atomic *glass* never *rest*

Dearest   *deceitful*   *depression,*
Will you restart this rusty heart without tearing apart the glue? I restricted foolish girls from ever entering. Protection provided by complex combinations with key. How did you break in and wreck the place? You bastard depression - never cease to erase damage that can't be undone with a double-cross hold. Truth be told ...I'm getting tired of pushing and pilling you out with no success. Instead, force fed failure to repress. The doctors have turned us into legal junkies, but do I care as much as they do about money?

Dearest   *devout*   *heart,*
Where do I begin to start that apology again? My abuse remains broken inside to hide from all to see. For you I count the steps and breath in a circulatory system that now feels like the coldest circuitry - a row of broken capacitors that each disaster struck. The warmest blood stuck in the loneliest valve of loves hemispheres that first appear to be normal on insurance of EKG's, until the bills crawled up my ass to bite me. Sorry my darling heart. Will you ever forgive thee?

Dearest   *diseased*   *brain,*
Is it my stress and strain of imbalanced chemicals dancing into erotic rhythm in once passive systems? Works of words such as anxiety, act, and addiction ring inside you. Simple reminders of who we now are; collected like trophies made way below heaven. Watch how easily the sadness really sits. Emotions decay too with damaging results that halt what I called in childhood, "The simplicity of happiness." Is this my fault? And the nervousness constantly comes undone. I tried to ravel it back in a unalarmed position, but instead my hands made the most insane noose executed with the most perfect

precisions ever I've made. Fragile little brain ... What will you make me destroy today as I walk towards the endless bay of the sea. Not stopping. No instructions. Now please, let me be.

Living Disorder

I would talk to the public if we weren't so jaded.
I saw you glace back at me, but that human feeling faded.
It doesn't matter where I go acceptance will never happen.
The people outside have secret codes; in bars, in packed cars,
on the street … but no one bothers me.
Well then fuck you, but it's not your fault.
You're too busy applying salt to the wound.
If it's a girl, they're assuming rape.
Why you gotta be such a little bitch?
Those young guys today need constraints!
WTF? Did your parents beat you with a wrench?
Don't stare too hard though - I got problems of my own.
I'm not ready for any compromises yet.
I'm never a threat, but people walk around me ... as if
I could go up in flames.
Like a soulless bomb; how insane is that?
May I ask?
Is it my personality?
My awkward face, the way I dress,
or just the way I stand up for myself?
Is it my music, phrasing, words I use to describe you
and the world?
Is it because I want to be close with strangers at night?
My big nose and unkempt hair;
my nasal voice or the way my fingers mess with the air?
You call me strange, but look at the shit around you.
Maybe neither of us will win this world with affection.
It's been years since someone took me seriously,
though I've been delirious my whole ridged life.
Will you be my friend if I pretend not to like you,
turning every event into a testosterone test?
Yes .... no one wants to admit;
they are one fucked up son of a bitch.

WE Town HO

By the hills I sweep the cars into the parkway
by movie stars and grand avenue hay days.
Mulholland drive suicides, James Dean,
and massive mud slides flowing through Hollywood,
Sunset drives, and white town by her side.
The people brush free from tangled mess,
and hooker pubic hair underwear.
No hustler expects any less than this moment,
to be a single flair.

oh cell phone …

oh cell phone …

You stupid Hollywood fakes
with your plastic face and blond hair looks -
wigs out of place and your rubber boobs;
a land of hard core noses.
Take a damn sniff, you sure ain't smelling roses;
you're smelling my ass ...
and I forgot to wipe.

Everyday I walk down the Blvd's.
Everywhere I go people need a quarter, a dime or two,
a cigarette, and by the time I'm home I have the blues.
Santa Monica, what a good ole place.
I wonder if there are as many Jews in outer space?
When I'm bumming hard I'll just go to the beach,
and eat a fucking rotten recycled peach.
If I had the fucking money,
I'd pay a bum a gram or two to suck my feet.

oh. oh. oh. Oh!

oh cell phone

chemical balances of the soul

I've trapped myself with addictions
that recorder my thought processes,
into macro codes in dreams deciphered
under the stupor of low dose toxins.
My work becomes a dull sleep of purgatory senses.
Never quite the same place twice when
I'm troubled with irrational sadness.
It takes over me, and dispenses friends at once.
I have to admit … I just may fucking hate everyone.
It's a dramatic start of weekdays that I now call empty time.
By the clock my mobile free weekends start, I encompass
the state of reflecting nothing but vanishing points.
Sometimes mumbled "effergy" from my crispy lips;
meaning "days the hours do not meet",
"day without meaning", or simply "day of no light".
Days it doesn't matter if you are conscious or beginning
to dream from the worthless sleep,
the misery seems to follow both lives you lead.
The question becomes blunt and dismal.
"Which one do you like better?"
"Which one would you rather live?"
I fell asleep that mid day.
I made fun of myself the other night
which gave me a guilty pleasure,
but he stood there close to crying
and cussing how wicked my ways have come,
all the times I've tried
to die by ways of pills laced with lye.
Is there any word or idea that comes
to mind that aren't lies?
I've been calm and conscious with strangers in general,
but it's times like these
I'm not adored with our world.

idiotalic

The brain I hold is done for.
My emotional peak came in 1st grade,
my mental at 27.
Ten years have passed down to a retardation,
halting to a rough dull stop of pathetic reasoning
of what's cognitive, what is fluid intelligence.
It slipped out a year ago,
but I can't remember what I don't have.
It's horrible.
I feel they are all laughing at me in exotical language.
"Look at that southern idiot!"
I feel the truth in this statement,
yet all I can do is sigh and grunt.
Once talented, once half bright,
now a poopsicle stick of sludge.

I'm so dumb,
I couldn't teach a genius how to walk a strait line.
I'm so dumb,
that my jokes are actually lazy paradoxes thrown with
improper rhyme,
but we are in the same.

I missed the gene pool with a quick escape from the institution
of intuition.
Too messed up to care; too f'ed to fight; too slow to play -
what good am I anymore?
I'm the Windows 98' CD exposed to high heat on that filthy
thrift store shelf.

I've turned into every vice of my parent's parents.
Every bad trait concentrated during my conception,
and nothing harsh skipped my generation.

The simplistic kept my vessel impaired, led strait,
but not enough to wipe all past memories.
The painful reminder of all the shit I used to comprehend.
Then the mind slips a little more.

What was I ranting about?
I don't remember, but I feel pretty pissed off!

personal overtures

The time ran out
and I marched through the sound of steady tapping
into a beat of subversive rapping all along the stretch of nylon
string.

My body moved soft then hard as elastic stretches into voids -
confused all by redoxing white noise.
I thought to myself, "I can see the end, can bring a friend,
everything will be alright."

They know of this pressure that beats like a heart -
then finally tears apart; give it all back I swear.

My sin, this skin at the end of the road is used, abused,
each hung from soiled rope.
I'm angry at this place, living in disgrace,
still marching though the sound of steady tapping
into a beat of revolution rapping all along the stretch of nylon
string.

Create modesty from fears
For that the king of the earth is dead
The world's a bomb

Our sky parts – soon turns red
It was a violent march
Of who is saved, and who's left dying

This we call the rotting stage
Whom pacifies us into the sultry
Sweat on dialect stones
Carved once by the wicked

We call home a hell to heaven
Starts a paradise

We cannot win without
The Name of whom we trust
Who of us disobey

Don't push that shit in my ear
Too far from removable
We are what we eat
So we become too sick like rats
Then give excuses and start the complaints

Again with the order of the day

Watch what you say and preach
For you don't know
Which invisible is watching
Without the intent
Of their own routine faith

Don't deliver to me after
When all is too late to rapture
Again with the same old day in
365 ways to say a name

It appears the blessing
Integrated with a curse
And I understand
That it must exist this way

We can't all be completely alone
No matter how still the time
There is none without our motions in bind

I came back into the line of noise
No friends to meet
Alone without a greeting
Found nothing personal left in me

user number selections
(prelude to shortly mad world)

saline drip, microchip;
in caved-in cities full of girls with big tits
lived alone far from those who are pretty.
waited four hours and forty-four minutes ...

it's in the 60's of vinyl nights
or 7% of what i might write

that's not too bad …

living in humility well
of 1% in 2012

shortly mad world to you
today was expected -
yet never the events that occurred
of course you remember when ...
you sacrificed a piggy float
in the middle of a joyous parade;
then rowed away on a boat made of people,
once your friends, but just skeletons today.

took yourself on a wonderful trip,
but i must admit, that no nerve is thin.
already in need of another klonopin.
open that beautiful mouth
so i can stuff it with shit.
taste ones dental fillings,
touch the tip of sweetly bitter numb.
tongues keep swirling around private ses-pools -
daily garbage incinerated in public exchanges,
and vials of unhealthy cum.

can you keep a secret?

of course you cant ...
well anyway,
hogs squeaks with protein oil leaks.
sharpened blades with sugar
to keep the wet slop sweet.
we wrap the meat in over-tanned ball sacs.
stays fresh til winter -

… that dreadful time sobriety has tracked me down,
to every step of my feet.
reducing a breath;
my chest involuntarily sinks.
slow movement of a jarring stupor
cracks my jaw to grinding teeth
wearing from bloody gums receded.
hopeless in half waken cells,
and momentary lapses;
comforted lassos greeted.
Sadness too violent for crying;
too edgy to break a panicked mood,
with docile pills overused.

anxiety meds in a 2016 vending machine;
pusher #-probing member touching paraffin waxy hand.
whats the fucking combination key code?
a tetrahexel button grid of characters add new anxieties as well,
filled skips and jumps soiled again.
making deals with visible device complexities,
offering stolen rx accounts and honey nectar for its heat sinks.
you spread it thinner and thinner;
butter appendages.
magic microphone machine dr. says,
"have a meddy day!"
i took a bow, and gave it one last stare,
before stuttering their numbers and names.

Future Sobriety Failure

It's driving me crazy - the way you talk
the way you walk - the way you're surprised
at all the things I can do ...
But I'd rather be embarrassed
about what I can't do, than be with you.

Riots and rain busted my bike
into fragments of dust one night.
Naked men swing their penis like a bat
to protect the chicken egg and turkey deluxe.
Baste my breast and call me Shirley
to expect what cums out early.
Baseball bats limp from the sound of lightning,
and tore apart my 800 speed Huffy.

Once I was sane but now I'm nuts.
Come to the garage and snort my cigarette butts.
I was alive before but now an empty glass,
so come to my house, and fill up my lonely ass.

Prone, stoned, broken enhanced -
I can't stand when you give me another
chance to sleep with your sisters.
They think the end is coming, but
I'm unfortunately doubtful.
Lets wait to see if the water rises,
and takes us away to a perverted island
before all is wasted.

Lift me high to heaven (please)

Dear God, I've been so bad
I lay in bed all day feeling sad
I cry me eyes out before I sleep
Waking up with a cooked turkey
My arm in its ass about a foot deep

Beautiful fried Chicken skins Oh Chicken Skins
Colonel Sanders was a greasy golden idol
until prophets struck the old man down
Oh sweaty Chicken Skins
Glorious golden Chicken Skins
I put my faith in a greasy bucket
so the rapture just may let me drown

Dear Guardian Angel, do you get bored
when I just stay in my little sad room?
Peeing in bottles that stay year round
never ending cupcake crumbs fall to the ground
I stuff my face till my belly is wrecked
while thinking of the girl I lost to that effect

I can't stop smoking blunts next to me stack of porns
wasting away my share in half millions of newborns
cum stained glass windows reach my peak in faith
if one day I'd just go outside and play
but now I weigh 666 pounds and
cant move out of my own shit stains
so here come the large humiliating cranes
that will *lift me high to heaven (please)*

Oh Chicken Skins, Oh sweaty Chicken Skins
We made a sacred pact to get married
Mary, - who's Mary? I don't care
As long as greasy thighs, Chicken Skin,

and God stand by her side
Oh please hear me Lord, and forgive these Chicken Skins ...
that I cannot decline

When you got a good friend

The dopers are different in chemistry.
We are naturally nice when not sober.
Indifferent and weak
when toxins dry out in wet pathogens.

I think back when I was blue,
missing the simplicity of happiness
before the sores of socializing grabbed me by new grown pubic
hairs in public school.

I tried to fit in, and held drugs
passed in my direction.
Guess it failed since the routine holds 27 years later.
A factor has disappeared from my statement above.

Now I have no one to fit with.
Not anyone.
I've become a star peg of dissipation -
common genius, what's your verification?

Too strange for typical company,
too plain for creeps.
No wonder I have this self taught distemperment.
Thought back to when I was blue today
and fucking got an evil eye.

Kills me when I'm not a good boy for you,
anyway I tried.
Told me to take my shit,
said "adieu.";
how well I know this impromptu.
I can't abide the formaldehyde itch that burns
you fucking son of a bitch.

Don't look at me weird fuck face -
I'm more mentally displaced that you know.
Not that I was in the progress in making a scene nor show.

Hey kid, stop staring!
I'm not your father.
If I am then I'm sorry for bothering you.
But just in case …
here's a half truth and a question.
If you end up like me, you chose the wrong path.
If not … could you let me stay at your moms flat?

my early lil' alzheimer haircut

i feel it. those awful misfired impulses inside my folding mass of mouse cheese carved from the early moon of videography. I collect them in 35mm tins with rust and prehistoric optical numbers that peak above newly created zeros. wait. where was i?

oh yes …

i'm seeing things with packs of nicotine my system bothers.
a fluid seems to come close to ahead,
yet i'm not recognizing the words you sing to me –
then calmly they're read.
i'm regretting what i remember from the past
no matter how insignificant my decisions came to.
was there too much THC while my body thrives off nicotine,
and caffeine drinks, SSRI's, with Clonazepam peaks?
perhaps i should have done more LSD,
during those ADHD days i used to watch television,
and record old re-runs of WKRP.

Wicked-Killings-Regarding-Paxil broke news on the radio.

i demanded my mind back, but only offered me more pills.
took a few to save my soul, and what else is new?
yes. it's a dreadfully lonely life
with an inhospitable little wife that no longer looks at you.
what i have left is what i remember.
the way reminded myself looking back at pages wrote,
and tapes once running in real time circulation.
clockwise specifications in transcriptions
realized and decoded separately by each ear, and shit …
they say the same damn thing each year.

stubborn asshole (on the ground)

Pilots play pretend we have turbulence.
Glad I'm on the ground.

Radicals take control and shoot passengers randomly.
Glad I'm in a car.

A 747 crashes in the mountains heading from Hobby to L.A.X.
- Everyone's dead.
Glad I decided to drive instead.

I get a text and fucking die in a car wreck,
still, glad I wasn't flying.

sam, i like ike

her eyes are a brilliant revolution
infinite portraits to classical solution
sensual seducing stares slip slowly
sam, push your turn hard into a wall
now we have prayers stranger than fiction
hold the truth that nothing is contradiction

her mind goes wild as she smokes the trees
there's nothing quite like it - watching you scream at the sea
with a strange list while paper presses against her leaves
now i push my turn into a wall harder than ever
she rides two bicycles during hurricane weather
don't shove your relative view, einstein had no clue
that static interference is what she sings
like the loop of a middle finger ring,
but now i must leave her alone -
for that things are quiet;
the city of austin has taken her heart

i wont blink for a second; time is closer than remembered
hold her hand in dark fallout shelters
after all, missiles may be coming along the shoreline dr.
think when the sunset never returns to cycle cellos and rifles
take a stand with recitals

lets pray with lip lock; strangled legs up in arms
lets pray with spanking tools and piano wire bruises
please knock me unconscious before i do to you over and over
again, into kinky repeaters

its not law, its love that i carry

times of Hurricane Ike

s a v e d

i don't give a shit about the politics of this.
i don't give a fuck about living in a rut.

would you people show,
another round of applause on me?

if i could turn it all around i would,
but just a little differently.

edrimefa-plic'nike'

placement - displacement -
ringing the numbers in all wrong.
tastement, in my basement -
laying cement foundations song.
to my head -
through a brain
instead, insane
in a closed case,
to the post race
i locked it up again
and to coke - a vein
it broke - it rained
in my next place
in a world waste ...
i played this song again

edrimefficane

placement - displacement - ringing the numbers in all wrong.
tastement, in my basement - laying cement foundation song.
to my head - through a brain
instead - insane
in a closed case
to the post race
i locked it up again
and to coke - a vein
it broke, it rained
in my next place, in a world waste
i cant do this song again.